Clem Sunter

FLAG
watching

How a fox decodes the future

TAFELBERG

Tafelberg, an imprint of NB Publishers,
a division of Media24 Boeke (Pty) Ltd,
40 Heerengracht, Cape Town, South Africa
www.tafelberg.com

Set in 11.5 on 14 pt Palatino
Cover and book design by Nazli Jacobs
Edited by Andrea Weiss
Proofread by Riaan de Villiers

⬯
Printed by **paarlmedia**, a division of Novus Holdings
First edition, first printing 2015

ISBN: 9780624076162
Epub: 9780624076179
Mobi: 9780624076186

To my beautiful family of Margaret,
Katy, Robert and David

Contents

Chapter 3

Chapter 1
From scenario planning to flagwatching

This book is based on a series of presentations that I have been making around South Africa and overseas. Because of the enthusiastic endorsement of the content of the talk from the audiences I addressed, I decided to turn it into a written text. The book has three objectives:

- to show the readers how to decode the secrets of the future by choosing the right flags to watch;
- to identify some of the flags that are transforming the global game and offer scenarios to 2020 for the global economy; and
- to outline the formula for a winning nation and provide a range of flags and scenarios that give an indication of whether South Africa will become one.

Before doing that I would like to reflect on my experience in the field of studying the future, so that it provides a context for my recommendations. Rather like the future itself, it has been a long and winding road with successes and setbacks along the way. As you will see, I did not choose to be a futurist. I was in a room, as a young man of 37, listening to an engrossing talk on a subject I had never heard about before, from a man I had never met before. Little did I know that my life was about to change for ever. That is the way it is and the way it will continue to be.

The history of the High Road

The story starts in the early 1980s. My company, Anglo American, was at the time the largest mining group in the world. As a result of poor forecasting of commodity prices during the 1970s, we were looking around for another way of handling the future.

We heard that Royal Dutch Shell had a process called scenario planning which they had used with great effect in capturing the two oil price shocks in the 1970s, when the oil price had suddenly jumped in the early and late parts of the decade. We asked the head of scenario planning at Shell to come out to Johannesburg and give us a presentation on the new methodology. His name was Pierre Wack, he was French and he was at the point of retiring from Shell.

He gave the Executive Committee of Anglo a presentation at our offices at 44 Main Street in Johannesburg. I, as the secretary to the Executive Committee, attended the meeting. The audience was blown away by Pierre, not only by the content of his talk, but by the way he gave it so enthusiastically and with such a bewitching accent. He looked like a futurist and his hands were a moving sculpture of his thoughts. Before he spoke, he asked if he could light up. Being French, we thought he was about to smoke a Gauloises cigarette, instead of which he produced two incense sticks, lit them, held them under his nostrils and said that he could think more clearly about the future if he was smelling incense.

That action meant he was hired on the spot. At the end of the session our Chairman, Gavin Relly, looked around the room and his eye fell on me. He said: "Clem, I would like you to take on the responsibility of introducing scenario planning into Anglo with Pierre as a consultant."

For me, this was a great surprise as I was just getting used to a normal mining career. Nevertheless, it sounded exciting and Pierre duly arrived with his colleague, Ted Newland, also a former member of the Shell planning department. We formed teams in London and Johannesburg and away we went, with the team in London looking at global economic scenarios and the team in Johannesburg concentrating on South Africa.

In late 1985, our work culminated in a presentation that I was asked to give around companies in our group entitled "The World and South Africa in the 1990s". The presentation went down so well that I asked Gavin Relly whether I could do a public presentation at an Indaba being held in Durban in June 1986. He generously agreed and off I went to Durban. I gave the presentation to an audience consisting of a diverse group of politicians and business people and it was as though I had detonated a bomb.

The following day, my secretary received at least a dozen calls from people at the conference asking me to repeat the talk to their particular constituency. Again, Gavin gave me time off and thus began a roadshow which lasted until the middle of the following year. Together with two of my colleagues, Mike Spicer and Jim Buys, we covered audiences totalling 25 000 around the country. A book I wrote on the talk topped the local charts in 1987 and a video was second to Michael Jackson's *Thriller* in the shops.

At the centre of the presentation was the slide illustrated on the next page. It was devised by Michael O'Dowd and Bobby Godsell who were members of the South African team. They built on the work of Edouard Parker, a French nuclear physicist who was also a friend of Pierre, and who subsequently turned his versatile mind to country risk analysis.

The diagram showed two possible paths that South Africa could take into the future: The 'High Road' of negotiation with the real leaders ending up in a settlement, a new constitution and a truly democratic election; or the 'Low Road' of co-opting some tame black representatives into a phony

Group
Individual
Transitional
Individual
Group

High
Growth

'OLD
WHITE
SA'
☆

Negotiation

'SWITZERLAND'
☆

Alliances

Co-option

Democratic Welfare

Nationalist
Power

Failure of
Growth

Distributist

Developed
Country

Low
Growth

PRESENT

Authoritarian

Negative
Growth

Waste
Land

Regional

Conflict

tricameral parliament which no one accepted, ushering in a period of violent conflict that could lead South Africa into a wasteland. The circle in the middle, dubbed the 'Argentinian Tango', was an alternative Low Road scenario where the country lurched between fascism and populism in a vain attempt to keep afloat.

Prophetically, the diagram also signified that there was a second crossroads around 20 years after the first one, where failure of economic growth could undo all the political progress made on the High Road. That is exactly where we are now.

The exercise proved the worth of scenario planning, since no forecast could have captured the release of Nelson Mandela and the sequence of events after it. But you could write a story about it, which is what a scenario is. You could capture a remote possibility, which became a probability and then a reality, even sooner than our team anticipated. Moreover you could use the High Road scenario, with the juxtaposition of the Low Road, to influence attitudes and change the conversation at the time.

Among the 25 000 to whom we made presentations were FW de Klerk and the Cabinet in November 1986. I always remember De Klerk turning to Pik Botha at the end of the presentation and asking: "Do you think this guy is for real?" Pik, bless his cotton socks, responded: "Yes, and I think he and his colleagues should talk to our MPs and government departments as well." We did.

Shortly thereafter, I lectured the Broederbond in the auditorium at the Rand Afrikaans University and later addressed Mangosuthu Buthelezi and his ministers in Ulundi, KwaZulu-Natal. He paid me the compliment of calling me his *sangoma*.

In January 1990, I visited Nelson Mandela in prison to discuss the future with him just before his release in February that year. I was told by a senior member of the ANC in exile that they watched the *High Road* video in Lusaka. In other words, most of the parties contending for power were covered in terms of exposure to our scenarios.

Interestingly, my mother in England used to ring me and say I had no right to tell South Africans about their future because I was not born there. My response was: "Mummy, people are listening and as long as they listen, I will present my message to them." One interesting session was with the police generals at a training camp in the Northern Transvaal as it was then known. Before the talk, I had tea with the commandant of the camp who had a sign on his desk which proclaimed: "Hit first, hit hard, hit everywhere." My immediate thought was that I was about to give a lecture on negotiating with the enemy, a slightly different tactic. Retrospectively, I think my coming from another country was in my favour as I was not seen as a traitor by ordinary folk.

In the end it is hard to tell how much the scenarios influenced the subsequent course of events because change was already in the air. People were concerned. The stellar reaction to our presentation, though, suggests that our scenario team was in the right place at the right time. It also showed that you have to put as much effort into disseminating the scenarios as into writing them, something that others in the field forget.

Indeed, the exercise was quoted by the American Peter Schwartz in his book *The Art of the Long View* – regarded as one of the best books ever written on scenario planning – as a great example of using scenarios to create a shared language. After reminding readers of Pierre's understanding that a scenario presentation should be a type of theatre, Peter said that the names High Road and Low Road gave the "polarised people of South Africa a common language for talking about their common future". I could not have put it better myself; and I agree with Pierre and Peter that knowledge is best imparted with a slice of humour and entertainment.

International observers called South Africa's peaceful transition to a new democracy a political miracle. They were fixated on the assumption that the only way change would come about was through a further tightening of sanctions against the country or, worse still, the kind of violent uprising that happened in Zimbabwe. Little did they know how much the odds were shifting towards our High Road scenario and away from the Low Road, as a result of all the remarkable people on both sides involved in negotiating a peaceful settlement.

However, fortune also favours the brave. The purpose of the global side of my presentation was to provide a plausible context for considering the possibilities for South Africa. One of the global scenarios our London team painted was called 'Imperial Twilight'. Its theme was the continuation of the arms race which would virtually bankrupt the Soviet Union. Apart from saying that the scenario was therefore unsustainable in the long run, I did make the following statement in the book: "Gorbachev could in the end fundamentally change the Soviet system."

Well, he did, and it led to Glasnost, the fall of the Berlin Wall in 1989 and the dissolution of the Soviet Union in the early 1990s. These events on the other side of the world were fortuitously timed because they coincided with the beginning of the transition in South Africa. I do not think that the National Party would have taken the High Road of negotiation seriously if the Soviet Union had remained as it was, namely an intact military bloc that constituted a high-level threat. The worst case scenario under a black government had always been that we would become a communist state and a vassal of the East. Reds under the beds was a big fear at the time. The gate opened in Moscow and the rest, as they say, was history in South Africa.

One final takeaway from the work we did was that it was more persuasive to offer the alternatives of the High Road and Low Road to South Africans and say "take your pick", rather than to wag our fingers and say "there is no alternative". That is the charm of scenarios. They are not prescriptive. They give people a sufficient degree of freedom to choose, so they do not feel put upon or that they are listening to propaganda being peddled by a particular interest group. One is opening minds to possibilities, not ramming a single message home.

The big 'however'

However, despite its success in altering the national debate, the process never really took off inside my company, Anglo American. It was never seen as part and parcel of the strategic planning process, but more like an exotic cabaret act which entertained and enlightened employees. Moreover, Pierre used to state unequivocally that scenario planners should stick to changing the 'microcosm' of the decision makers, namely how they viewed the surrounding environment, by using memorable language. But what scenario planners should not do is trespass into the territory of actually considering options and making decisions. That was management's preserve.

Pierre himself did some interesting work for us on the gold market as our mines were collectively the biggest producer of gold in the world. He concluded that gold was the most unpredictable metal of all since there were so many driving forces behind the price. He spoke of the gold price being like a railway carriage hooked behind a different locomotive every month. One month the locomotive would be demand by investors and speculators; next month it would be the needs of jewellery manufacturers and other industries using gold as a raw material; and then suddenly the central banks would become major players in the market on both the buying and selling side.

He also gave De Beers, our sister company, some valuable insights into the future of natural and synthetic diamonds. Yet, when he retired from being a consultant to our group in the 1990s, the scenario process came to a grinding halt. The teams were disbanded and although we did one or two workshops around specific issues of interest to management, to all intents and purposes the discipline was dead and buried.

I was terribly disappointed by this turn of events which, even as a scenario planner, I did not anticipate. I even remember two fairly cynical comments made by members of our board who obviously believed the function was of little value to the real world of business: "Scenario planning should be something you should do in your spare time" and "The only point of scenario planning is to be one month ahead of *The Economist*".

At this stage, I had already moved on to be Chairman and CEO of Anglo's Gold and Uranium Division, but the failure haunted me. I could not get over the fact that we had had such enormous success on the national platform, but at company level our team was considered irrelevant. Of some comfort were Pierre's words of praise for our exercise: "I changed the mindset of Shell but you guys changed the mindset of a nation. *C'est magnifique!*"

I still gave some public lectures on the scenario approach and also kept in touch with Pierre and his circle of remarkable futurists – swapping information here and there. But even in the division of which I was head, I had lost so much confidence that I did not think it was appropriate to reintroduce the classical model of scenario planning as part of examining the future of our mines and shafts. And that was despite knowing that all five-year plans and forecasts that companies produce are not worth the paper they are written on. Their assumptions, particularly relating to product prices, are blown away within six months.

Meanwhile, on the national front several splendid exercises were done by other organisations, including the famous Mont Fleur scenarios on the future of the South African economy. One was named 'Icarus' to denote the idea that if you flew too close to the sun of populism, you were bound to fall out of the sky. The economy would boom, then bust. Another was called 'The Flight of the Flamingos' to highlight the theme that a winning nation and economy was very much a co-operative affair between the state and private sector, where they drew strength from each other. Noteworthy was the fact that some of the participants were to become key economic players in the new dispensation and they admitted that the Mont Fleur adventure had influenced their subsequent thinking. This was something new. The scenarios were not written by a professional team in isolation and then presented to the decision makers. The latter played a prominent role in formulating the scenarios.

Three game-changing encounters

My life is no different to anybody else's in that turning points come out of the blue. I had three of them. The first one occurred in the summer of 1966. I had completed my degree at a university in England and happened to be on holiday in a place called Rock in Cornwall. I needed a crew for a dinghy race in the estuary and there was a girl sitting on a wall outside the local pub. I asked her to crew for me and she accepted. Needless to say, we came last in the race as I am no expert on the tiller, but she did ask me back for dinner with her parents. Her father was Managing Director of Charter Consolidated, a subsidiary of Anglo American in London. My life changed that evening as three months later, after an interview at their offices in Holborn Viaduct, I joined Charter as a management trainee.

Soon thereafter I met my future wife in the office (she was not the crew member) and that was to be the second game-changing encounter. In 1971, 18 months after being married, we moved to Zambia because she wanted me to experience Africa, as she was born in Pretoria and raised north of the border in Mazoe. I was then transferred to Anglo's office in Johannesburg in 1973 and have been in South Africa ever since. Incidentally, this is my 49th year with Anglo, where I now serve as a non-executive on the South African board and my 46th year of marriage! How is that for a change in direction from possibly being a stockbroker in London like my father? I hope I have convinced you that life is a series of crossroads which you come upon by chance and the challenge is to make the right choice at each intersection. Personally, I have no regrets.

However, I must return to the purpose of this book. The

third encounter was when I was sent a thesis by a young woman who was studying for an Executive MBA at the Graduate School of Business in Cape Town. Her name is Chantell Ilbury and her thesis was on scenario planning, particularly as it pertained to small business. She wanted me to look over it before submitting it to her professor. This was a game-changer as she made two points that strongly resonated with me, given my previous experience at Anglo.

Firstly, she said that the whole technique was far too abstract and intellectual to appeal to ordinary business people, especially entrepreneurs. I could vouch for that. In the 1980s, I used to go to Shell's head office in London, overlooking the Thames, to compare the Anglo global scenarios with Shell's. I would say to the concierge on the ground floor, "I'm here to see the scenario planning team." He was wont to throw his eyes in the air and respond: "You mean the priests of the Nile?" The sheer intellectual brilliance and academic qualifications of many of the team set them apart from the normal mortals in the management ranks. Shell is still the Holy Grail of scenario planning, but it comes at a cost. Like the criticism I got in Anglo, I remember one Shell operational head wryly observing that people who have heavenly thoughts were of no earthly use.

The second point that Chantell made was that scenario planning on its own was just day dreaming. You have to gauge the impact of each scenario on you, your family, your business, whatever or whomever is close to you. Then, based on the impact and probability of the scenario, you must decide what you are going to do about it in handling the challenges it poses. You must connect all the dots and not just gaze at the future for its own sake.

Pierre would have agreed and disagreed with this sentiment. On the one hand, he felt that scenarios that did not persuade decision makers to change their course of action were a waste of time. On the other hand, he did not believe it was in the remit of a scenario planner to consider the options available to chase the opportunities and counter the threats offered by the scenarios. That was management's responsibility and, at the highest level, the prerogative of the board of directors. He actually told me that at one time in Shell he had indulged in option planning, but it had not gone down well with top management who felt he was trespassing on their territory.

Moreover, he used another argument against getting involved in options: It raises the temptation of producing scenarios which suit the existing strategy of the business. In plain English, you put the cart before the horse and write scenarios with the end result in mind, namely a desirable future well within the comfort zone of all the recipients making the decisions. Therefore, it is best not to put yourself in their shoes. Rather stay on the outside as an independent advisor and use familiar language to connect with them. The mistake is to immerse yourself so deeply in their management dilemmas that you become one of them. That is when you lose your objectivity.

Enter the fox

I felt that even with Pierre's misgivings about linking scenarios to options and selling your soul as an insider, there was room for a more practical model. To put scenario planning on the map with ordinary people required some kind of parallel process to the cognitive skills they used on a daily basis to meet the uncertainties occurring in their lives. Chantell had the same thoughts and we decided to write a book exploring a new model. We called it *The Mind of a Fox*. It took us five months to write and it was published in June 2001.

We selected the title for a particular reason. The great British philosopher Isaiah Berlin's metaphor of the hedgehog and the fox suited the message we were trying to get across. He distinguished between hedgehogs, with one big idea in their head to the exclusion of all other ideas (a mental state Jim Collins recommends in his more recently published book *Good to Great*), and foxes, with many different ideas that are small enough not to dominate each other. The hedgehog/fox terminology actually originated in lines of verse written by an ancient Greek poet named Archilocus in around 650 BC, over 2 700 years ago. History does not relate why he chose these two animals.

While we accept the point about having a vision of what you want to do in life and focusing on it, it must not be too rigid. We reckoned scenario planners are more like foxes than hedgehogs because they spread their attention across multiple futures rather than bet on a single forecast. Consequently, they are more prepared to be flexible. Equally, foxes are animals with bright eyes to pick up any changes in the environment around them and possess the agility to respond to those changes in a quick fashion. That is as important to a business as is the quality of its vision, given that business games can go through vast shifts in a short space of time.

Charles Darwin, we felt, would have approved of our stand on the grounds that a Darwinian business behaves like a fox. It is the first to adapt to the changing reality. The subtitle of our book, "Scenario Planning in Action", emphasises the speedy implementation of new ideas conceived during the process of thinking like a fox.

The foxy matrix

The crux of *The Mind of a Fox* is the matrix shown on the next page.

The principles embodied in the matrix are as follows. First, use the classical model of scenario planning to look outwards at the world beyond your control and examine what

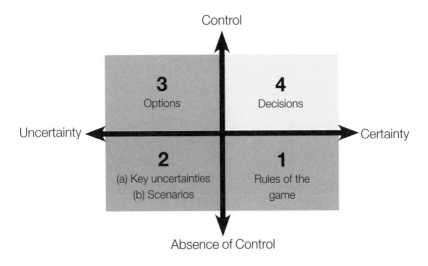

is certain and uncertain about it. Then look inwards at the options and decisions within your control to cope with the changes. Simple and straightforward, and it has proved a most popular technique, despite Pierre's reservations about not linking the bottom with the top of the matrix. You just have to be aware of not compromising your perception of the outside world with your ambitions and fears. You must take off your tinted glasses and wear transparent ones in order to be absolutely neutral about the incoming data.

Thousands of businesses around the world have downloaded our model from our website, www.mindofafox.com. It is a great agenda for having a strategic conversation about the state of your business and where it is headed. We make the point that after surveying the outside world, options fall into two categories: strategic options about creating a new direction for the business with new products and services, new geographies and new consumer markets, innovation being the critical driver; and tactical options about improving the productivity and efficiency of the business. We also emphasise that when you finally arrive at decisions, you must ask the question: Who is going to do what by when to make things happen? Execution of a plan is as important as its formulation.

I think it is the sheer simplicity of our matrix, and the common sense behind it, that has made it so popular. We have been told that our website is now one of the most frequented strategy websites on the internet, although one expert on these matters took a bit of the sheen away. He suggested that a large volume of our hits were due to the name of our site and were in fact men in search of foxy women. Perhaps we should change the name of our site to *Fifty Shades of Fox*!

9/11 and all that

At the outset, the book did not sell that well because books on scenario planning seldom do. Then something happened which propelled it on to the South African best seller list. According to one book chain, it was the number one seller of any title in 2002 and in 2003 it was number two because Harry Potter was number one. So what was the event? It was 9/11.

What we had done to demonstrate the power of our model was to include a formal letter to George Bush in the text at the time he first became US President. In it we intimated that if he wanted to leave a legacy, he would have to start thinking like a fox, capture some of the extreme futures that he might face as president and work out contingency plans. We nominated as his principal risk a massive terrorist strike on a Western city which would completely transform his presidency and consign the United States into a 'Gilded Cage' where it shut itself off from the rest of the world. It happened three months after we published the book.

These were our exact words: "But human ingenuity being what it is and necessity being the mother of invention, desperately poor people will always find a way of breaching your barricades."

Now we know that Osama Bin Laden came from a wealthy

background and Arab countries are not the poorest in the world. Nevertheless, the resentment against the richest country in the world was always there, especially among his followers who did not share in the material prosperity of the West. To this was added religious hatred as a motive.

Apparently, the Americans did a literature search within weeks of 9/11 and ours was the only book published anywhere in the world in 2001 before 11 September that anticipated this threat in a letter to the president. I even received a call on my mobile phone from someone purporting to be from the US State Department. To this day, I have wondered whether it was a friend of mine having me on with a fake American accent. I answered all the questions posed about the source of our material as honestly as I could. I also stated it was our job as scenario planners to look at things on the edge of the possible.

Thank heavens we did not mention New York and planes flying into buildings in the letter as we might be languishing in Cuba today. We talked of nuclear terrorism and somebody planting a nuclear device in the middle of a city. To quote: "You only need one terrorist organisation to hold the rich old millions to ransom by planting a hidden nuclear bomb in the middle of one city for everyone to realise that conventional military capability is useless against such a threat."

However, it does raise an important point. A fox will never capture the exact circumstances and timing of an event. For that you need inside knowledge. Yet you can capture the idea of an event and we had three flags to signify a terrorist attack on Western soil was in the offing.

The first flag was the growing confrontation between the major religions of the world, particularly Christianity, Islam and Judaism, which began in the late 1980s and intensified during the 1990s. Indeed, a Middle-Eastern expert who addressed an Anglo workshop in London in 1988 said that he had studied the teaching content at some of the fundamentalist schools in Saudi Arabia. His conclusion was that it was a recipe for war by the end of the century. It was no coincidence that 15 of the 19 suicide pilots were Saudi Arabian.

In a book I published in 1992 with the title of *The New Century*, I wrote the following: "The growth of fundamentalist Islam poses a serious challenge to Western lifestyles and values. This in itself is not a geopolitical problem. It only becomes one if attempts are made by zealots to impose Islam on countries wishing to pursue other paths of development. The attractions to the 'poor young billions' of a religion based on the strict code of the Koran are obvious. It anchors their existence in spiritual certainties when all is flux around them; it gives a clear sense of purpose in a world that for many has no meaning whatsoever; and it abhors materialism, a quality the poor do not possess anyway through force of circumstance. The Middle East, Pakistan, the southern republics of the former Soviet Union and northern Africa are all falling under the spell of fundamentalist Islam. That is a formidable area of influence. How much further it will spread and at what rate is unknown. Equally unknown is whether the spreading of an idea will degenerate into a war of beliefs. A nuclear *jihad* is not out of the question. Fundamentalist Islam is a wild card with the ability to alter the balance of power in important parts of the world."

Re-reading this passage, we are in this space today. Yet, political commentators in the UK are bewildered by British teenagers flying to Turkey to join Islamic State in Syria. One called it "utterly ludicrous". Prime Minister David Cameron has come out with a five-year plan to counter extremism, but young Muslim people have already said that integration cannot be a one-way street and trust takes a long time to develop.

The second flag for 9/11 was the increasing sophistication in the strategy and tactics of groups dedicated to the downfall of America in places like Afghanistan. Again this was a detectable trend in the 1990s as was the supply of more sophisticated equipment to these groups. It was largely ignored on Bill Clinton's watch as President when something could have been done about it.

The third flag could be classified as an event as opposed to a trend. It was the pair of attacks on American embassies in Kenya and Tanzania in 1998, which we believed was a dress rehearsal for the real thing in America.

Chantell and I have often thought that if we had been invited by American security agencies to give a presentation of our material to them, they would have recognised some of the genuine flags that they were in possession of, which we knew nothing about. It came out in the congressional enquiry after 9/11 that a young woman in the FBI had approached her boss on six occasions and said: "Sir, there's a flying school down the road where Arabs are learning to take off but not land." She was ignored on the grounds that Arabs were too incompetent to attack Americans on American soil, a deadly misassumption that a fox would have interrogated by offering alternative scenarios and flags.

So we could not have had our methodology verified in a more dramatic form than that and overnight we became quite big celebrities in the global field of futures study. As Pierre would have put it, we got it vaguely right rather than being precisely wrong. To us it indicated for the first time the importance of linking scenarios to flags and not just playing scenarios without flags.

It also showed that one has a better chance of turning an 'unknown unknown' – something you don't know you don't know – into a 'known unknown' or quantifiable risk if you are examining trends and events for potential flags. This requires a healthy dose of imagination to go along with intelligence and reasoning. 9/11 proved to us that black swan events can be captured in advance if you have chosen the right flags to watch.

We received an interesting comment from an American woman who bought our book at the airport to read on an overnight flight to New York on September 10, 2001. She finished it before she went to sleep, and subsequently recalled that the only thing she thought was ridiculously over the top was our suggestion that terrorism could redefine George Bush's presidency (the word 'terrorism'was only mentioned once in the lead-up to the 2000 US presidential election). Then she woke up to the announcement that the plane was being diverted because of a terrorist strike on the city.

I have to mention that, on the actual day of the strike, I was in Cape Town staying at a place called Ravenswood in Hatfield Street. It was the Anglo guest house. As I went upstairs in the late afternoon, I saw Anglo's medical head, Dr Brian Brink, watching the television in his room and stroking his chin very intently. He called me in and said that a plane had just crashed into the top of the World Trade Centre in New York. As he said it, the second plane hit the second building, proving that it was no accident but a terrorist event. A weird feeling came over me as I had to give a lecture that evening in Stellenbosch. After I read out the letter we had written to George Bush, several members of the audience quizzed me about how we foresaw such a thing. My answer was that the letter demonstrated that it was an idea expressed as a possibility, not a detailed prediction for which you need inside knowledge. That is a big difference. For good measure, I added that scenario thinking on these lines is something normal mortals can do if they buy into our approach.

Before leaving this issue, I subsequently met Rudi Giuliani who was the mayor of New York at the time of 9/11. He was out in South Africa to promote his book on leadership and I had been asked to open and close his session at Gallagher

Estate in Midrand, Gauteng. Afterwards we had lunch together, and he told me that a few months before 9/11 they had done a practice drill involving all the emergency and accident units to prepare for an aircraft accident in the city. Apparently, it is routine stuff done on an annual basis. On the day of 9/11, 14 794 of the 17 400 people occupying the two buildings at the time of the incident were evacuated and made it out. Of the 2 606 civilians that were killed, 90% were on or above the floors that were hit and could not be rescued. Sadly, around 414 firemen and other emergency personnel also died in the rescue operation.

My reaction was that the aftermath was handled superbly by the authorities, given the short time between the planes striking the two buildings and their collapse. There would have been far more casualties were it not for the preparedness of the emergency services. It was not an accidental air crash that they were called out for, but they had played scenarios that were vaguely right rather than precisely wrong.

The Socratic Method

After the success of *The Mind of a Fox*, we were not immune to being foxes ourselves. Both Chantell and I picked up new ideas from our clients, which suggested we should adapt our model.

We published *Games Foxes Play* in 2005 in which we expanded the original foxy matrix into a full-scale conversation model. We pursued the metaphor of business being a game that, in contrast to rugby, soccer or cricket, could transform itself into something entirely new every five to 10 years.

We followed up with *Socrates & the Fox* in 2007 which recommended that companies had to behave like Socrates by regularly going back to first principles and asking themselves: "Why do we exist? Are we still relevant, and if not, what are we going to do about it?"

We even included a mock encounter between Socrates and an articulate fox in some woods on the outskirts of Athens.

At one stage, the fox says: "Life can surprise you and it is better to be aware of the surprises in advance, or have a very fast reaction time if they really do come out of the blue. Don't you agree?" Socrates responds: "Of course; what you are does not determine what you will be."

At the end of the conversation he praises the fox as follows: "You see things as they really are and, by doing just that, you see into the future. My life's work has been trying to give people a fraction of your talent by asking questions that reveal the truth behind the mask of appearances."

In 2011, all three books were combined into *The Fox Trilogy*. In the introduction, we remarked on how important flags had become in signalling that a new scenario was coming into play. If properly used, they could assist in giving a subjective probability to a scenario depending on how much they had been raised. We also had as a subtitle to the book: "Imagining the unimaginable and dealing with it". Nobody imagined three years ahead of the 2008 global economic meltdown that we were heading for a crash which would rival the one which preceded the Great Depression of the 1930s. In *Games Foxes Play*, published in 2005, we sounded a warning of a turning point being reached as you will see in the next section. Socrates would have been proud.

Premonition of a downturn

In the chapter on scenarios in our second book, we highlighted the fact that the world economy could move from a 'Long Boom' scenario to a recession-linked scenario we called 'Hard Times'. We described the latter as follows: "This is a scenario of a normal economic downturn caused by the usual suspects of governments and consumers overextending themselves and building up an inordinate amount of debt, stock markets getting too greedy, companies installing too much extra production capacity, etc."

The flag for the shift from one scenario to the other was a decline in US property values as a result of which the majority of American consumers would stop spending because their principal asset, their house, was declining in value. This would trigger a retreat in the US economy, as two-thirds of it was represented by consumer spending.

In the last quarter of 2006, the Case-Shiller index – which measures property prices across the US – levelled out; and in January 2007 it began a fall which continued into the middle of the year. Accordingly, in mid-2007 we gave Hard Times a 50% probability, even as the stock market was continuing to rise, and made it neck-and-neck with Long Boom. When the Dow Jones Industrial Average started falling later in the year, we raised the probability of Hard Times further to 80% – a near certainty – and with the collapse of Lehman Brothers in September 2008 to 100% for 12 months. The scenario had become reality.

Please note, we did not choose the actual cause of the crash as a flag. It was a security class called sub-prime mortgages. We knew nothing about them in 2005. But our flag of declining property values was what exposed sub-prime mortgages for what they really were – loans that should never have been given in the first place. In a falling market, they were worthless even when they were bundled up into triple-A rated collateralised debt obligations (or CDOs). I would also add that we had no idea in advance of the degree of the wipe-out of value across all markets. It was massive.

Interestingly, in April 2006, I was asked to have an informal conversation, explaining our methodology, with members of the faculty at the Central Party School near Beijing. It is the leadership academy for the Chinese Communist Party and is responsible for developing China's five-year plans. I knew that the Chinese were worried about the financial condition of America since they were sitting on a huge stock of American treasury bonds. I therefore gave the aforementioned example of the use of property prices as a flag; so I have always wondered how much they remembered it when the financial crash actually happened 18 months later. Did it make them look more quickly at stimulatory measures to expand their internal economy to make up for the loss of exports to America? I don't know.

Pierre Wack himself had a great flag for a possible property crash in Japan when prices reached absurd levels in the late 1980s. At one stage the Emperor's palace in Tokyo was worth more than the entire state of California! His flag was a decline in golf club membership in and around Tokyo. His reasoning was that golf was a new craze for the Japanese and one of the last things they would give up. In 1989, membership numbers started declining and in 1990 the crash happened. Japan has never been the same since. In a similar vein, the rise and fall of gambling turnover in Macau is probably as good a flag as any to judge the immediate economic growth prospects of China.

The Business Gameboard

Judging from the enthusiasm of executive teams whose strategic sessions we have been facilitating in the last 15 years, the gem in our later portfolio is the 'Business Gameboard' shown on the next page.

Going from worst to best, if your company is in the 'Fubar' quadrant where the market is declining and you are no longer competitive, you should sell it, close it or administer major surgery on it. Spelt with an 'm' rather than an 'f', it means mucked up beyond all recognition. The 'f' version originated as military slang.

In the bottom right quadrant, 'Fool's Paradise' is where you

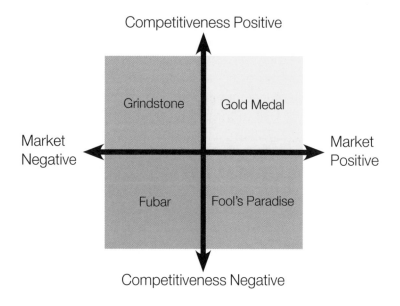

Competitiveness Positive

Grindstone | Gold Medal

Market Negative ← → Market Positive

Fubar | Fool's Paradise

Competitiveness Negative

are making money even though you are no longer competitive. The strength of the market covers up your weaknesses. Should the market turn down, you can end up fighting bankruptcy and death in the Fubar. On the top left hand side is the 'Grindstone' quadrant where the market is tough but you are making a profit by putting your nose to the grindstone and forever sharpening your competitiveness. However, you are concentrating so hard on efficiencies that you have little time for strategy. One client said that they were in the extreme version of Grindstone which they preferred to call 'Empty Wheels'. It is where the hamsters get so fatigued, they quit the wheel and watch it slowing down without their effort. Their drooping whiskers and shaking heads indicate their refusal to climb back on again. Many companies have retrenched so many staff in today's economic hard times that the long working hours and the stress induced on those that remain are sending them in that direction.

The last quadrant on the top right hand side is where we all want to be, namely 'Gold Medal'. You are the champion in innovation and efficiency to whom everybody else in the industry looks up. But even there the challenge is to maintain your edge and not become complacent. The tendency for many companies is to take their foot off the accelerator and fall into Fool's Paradise, or worse still Fubar, if the market turns down at the same time.

Good strategy is what moves you from left to right on the Business Gameboard because you are consistently coming up with new products to keep your market growing. Good tactics moves you from the bottom of the Business Gameboard to the top, with rising productivity, lower unit production costs and slicker production and marketing processes.

Many companies pull out our Business Gameboard every six months to see what movement they have made, either positively or negatively over the period. It is a very good reality check.

The curse of size

In a strategy session, we ask a client where they would locate their overall business on the Business Gameboard. Not only that, but where the momentum of the business is taking them in the future. If they are a group of businesses, we drill down and ask in which quadrant they would put their individual business units and sometimes we go even further down to individual products and services. The aim is to separate the dogs from the stars and decide what to do with the dogs, while chasing the stars.

In order to do all of this, you have to consider some specific flags such as the revenue and profit growth of the business, the state of the balance sheet, whether the cash flows are positive or negative, the improvement or decline in market share of your products and services and, particularly in mining, where the company stands in the 'cost per unit of output' league table of all the commodities it produces. But there are other flags that can move you in the blink of an eye from one quadrant to another such as the introduction of a revolutionary technology into the industry, competitors with a fresh approach, new legislation and changes in consumer taste. One minute you are king of the castle, next minute you are dethroned and descending into obscurity.

Now comes the rub. In our experience of doing over 1 500 sessions in the last 15 years, the bigger the company is, the more blind it is to the flags that are changing its business game. The flag can be right in front of management's eyes but they just ignore it for any number of reasons. Too much money is invested in the existing game, they are too emotionally attached to it or they are exercising the ostrich option of putting their head in the sand in the hope that the flag will disappear.

Take Kodak. As the world's leading camera manufacturer in 1978, they invented the digital camera. But at the time they had so much money invested in the film camera that they allowed competitors like Canon to take advantage of their very own invention. Kodak did not see their invention as a game-changer and now they are no more as a camera maker. You can however have your ID photograph taken at Kodak Express. The same applied much earlier to Western Union when they were offered the patent on the telephone for $100 000 by Alexander Graham Bell in 1876. They dismissed it as nothing but a toy, believing their telegram business was impregnable. At least, they diversified into other activities such as money transfers and are still around today.

Similar sentiments can be expressed about Nokia and Blackberry. At the top of their game, they did not see the lethal consequences of the smartphone for their business. Apple and Samsung came from nowhere to topple them. As one of our friends commented, elephants cannot be foxes and now Apple and Samsung are the elephants. Will they be toppled by the next generation of foxes?

Possibly, the best example where greed was the filter and screened out any idea of contrary flags was the great financial crash of 2008. Think of all those American banks on Wall Street, with the pick of Ivy League university graduates manning their trading desks, and how their delusions sent them into the Fubar quadrant where they had to be ignominiously rescued by the US Federal Reserve Bank. Hedgehogs supreme, they are now back to their old ways and, more importantly, their old bonuses. Here and there they have paid fines for malpractice – enough to sink most other businesses – but no CEO went to jail for gross negligence. Later on, I will be talking about the flags being raised in a zero-interest world of which they are again oblivious.

Outside of the business world, I can provide one other illustration of the tendency to ignore inconvenient flags. America's powerful gun lobby and the public devotion to the constitutional right to bear arms mean that Congress is virtually blind to two flags changing the game of mass homicide. Guns are becoming more lethal and sophisticated; and the number of people killed since 9/11 in non-terrorist-related incidents in the US far exceeds the number killed in terror acts. Yet, no congressman dares to tamper with the gun laws for fear of not being re-elected.

I guess that one of the general conclusions one must draw from these illustrations of ineptitude and unawareness is that very few companies stay in the Gold Medal quadrant for long. Their senses are dulled by their success and a fawning media; bureaucracy and inertia creep in; the original founding entrepreneurs leave and, in the absence of any succession planning, are replaced by unimaginative administrators; and the game moves on to new corporate players. The cycle of birth, adulthood and death is borne out in the changing composition of the Dow Jones and Footsie indexes listing the top 100 companies in the US and UK. Nations rise and fall and so do companies.

A formula for longevity

On reading the last few paragraphs, you must be thinking that there is no such thing as a sustainable business – the phrase much in vogue today. A company, even if it is lucky, is doomed to a lifetime cycle of early struggle, a breakthrough to rapid growth and a tapering-off which ends in oblivion. More or less like a human being, starting with infancy, young adulthood when you think you can live forever, maturity when you know you cannot, senility and finally death. The only difference is that the average lifespan of a business is a lot less than the average lifespan of a human being in a developed country. Moreover, the mortality rate of small first-time businesses is around 80% which is why failure has to be a learning experience.

Occasionally there are exceptions in the corporate kingdom, like General Electric and Ford Motor, which have been around for over a century and are still firing on all cylinders. In fact, in long-serving industries such as banking, oil and transport, examples of companies breaking the mould with a relatively durable existence are there. Equally, walk down any high street in the UK and you will find medium-sized and small family-owned shops handed down from generation to generation for even longer. Take a stroll in the countryside and the same thing is true of many family farms.

What is the secret to their longevity?

You might say in many instances not growing too large! However my answer is that long-lasting companies retain a foxy outlook with bright eyes scouring the environment – in this case the market – to detect any changes. They possess the flexibility to adapt their plans and the agility to carry them through after they've noticed the changes. A sustainable business is not, as you envisage in nature, a tranquil meadow full of slow-growing blossoms bathed by the sun and nurtured by the rain. It is a restless business, always on the prowl for new markets with new innovations; living its brand in exciting ways; and trying to offer a cheaper alternative by outsmarting its competitors in getting its product to the customer. Yes, the company needs to be honest, environmentally sensitive and treat its staff well to be called sustainable, but that is as far as it goes. Innovation is about being a constant source of disappointment to yourself and yearning for better.

As such, sustainable businesses know full well that a static condition will move them to the left on our Business Gameboard on account of declining sales and profit caused by obsolescence of their products. They recognise too that, without the latest technologies and management practices, they will retreat to the lower level of our Business Gameboard as their costs rise and efficiencies drop relative to their competitors. They know the ultimate destination through inaction is Fubar.

Were Charles Darwin alive today, he would be nodding his head in agreement while these opinions on how to extend your life as a business species were expressed. His phrase 'survival of the fittest' is often misinterpreted to mean survival of the most powerful animals in the neighbourhood. If you study his theory of evolution closely, he is actually referring to those species which fit in most with the changing requirements of nature by spontaneously adapting to it. They are the ones which survive for the longest time. The process of adaptation was considered by Darwin to be purely random as opposed to some kind of purposeful design. The lucky species which inherited the modified genes were preserved, while the rest were destroyed by natural selection. For a company, it is quite to the contrary; adaptation should be a deliberate strategy as the needs of the market, of individual consumers and of society in general, change. Otherwise, you die.

To conclude this section, I remember making a video in the 1990s for the American market entitled *Scenario Thinking: Multiple Pathways to the Future*. The producer was himself an American who had a history of putting fresh business ideas on the screen. One of the sequences we filmed at the beginning of the video had me standing on a railway track near Milnerton in Cape Town. Looking one way, there was a single track which represented the past. Looking the other way, the line split up into a multiple array of tracks after passing through a set of points. This represented the future.

In the middle of the shoot, a real train came out of a nearby tunnel on our line, much to the surprise of the producer who had been told this was a disused track. We had to remove ourselves and the equipment hurriedly from the train's path. Otherwise, we would have been 'fubarred' altogether. Our speed of response ensured our collective longevity. The producer and crew heaved a sigh of relief, and so did I. The only regret was that we did not capture it on film to illustrate how quick adaptation can be when your life is on the line.

The uncertainty of being

When people have asked me over the years what I do for a living, I normally respond that I have spent my life in the mining industry. Later on I became a scenario planner as an extra responsibility at the request of my employer. If the questioner is mystified by the term 'scenario planner', I go back to basics and say that I look at possible futures by composing stories of how they could pan out. I even mention that the origin of the word 'scenario' was a written outline of a film, novel or stage work giving details of the plot and individual scenes. In Hollywood, you peddled scenarios to film producers to get them to make a movie of your script. The word 'planning' was added after the word 'scenario' to convey the message that stories written by scenario planners were about the future.

Despite all this, some members of the public still confuse scenario planning with being a forecaster or prophet. Indeed, articles have appeared stating that Chantell and I predicted 9/11. We did not. We captured the idea in a scenario and added the flags to watch for an increase in probability. Only when you give 100% probability to a scenario can you be said to have converted it into a forecast. However, projecting a single line into the future to the exclusion of all other futures is something that can rarely be done, particularly in those fields involving human interaction such as politics and economics. There simply is not the level of certainty that surrounds $2 + 2 = 4$ or Isaac Newton's landmark discovery that, as night follows day, an apple will fall from a tree because of gravity.

Human affairs are much messier as emotion often trumps reason and randomness sends you up unexpected alleys. In other words, real life does not mix naturally with mathematics and science even though quantum physics is all about the unpredictable nature of elementary particles. Moreover, you can seldom rely on the past to act as a guide to the future, for as Pierre put it with a wry smile: "The future is seldom what it used to be!"

You might argue that the finger of fate or divine intervention from above determines much of what happens in the future. Then you are denying the existence of free will as an essential element of the human soul. You are also denying the role of chance when a croupier spins the roulette wheel. It is an uncomfortable thought that life has much in common with a casino and your choice may be right or wrong through sheer luck. A prophet may insist that he or she has a special access to the future through a direct link to a supernatural authority. That is fine by me but I do not possess such a link. Mind you, Pierre studied at an Indian Ashram to sharpen his spiritual insight and add another lens through which to look at the future.

I prefer to consider all the horses in the race before placing my bets. Then, as the race proceeds, the odds will change depending on the position of each horse at a particular moment in time. Even then, the horse at the back of the pack can put in a sensational run down the final stretch and win. Never rule out a wild-card scenario until the race is over. Despite thinking like a fox, you must be prepared to be wrong sometimes; but there is less chance of being wrong than a hedgehog putting all his money on a single prospect and sticking to it through thick and thin. Somebody asked me a few months ago whether this applies to life after death. Hmm!

The widespread practice of flagwatching

As a species, we are a fight or flight bunch. We jump to extinguish 'burning platforms' but don't react well to slow-moving threats. The well-known analogy of a frog jumping out of boiling water but dying in water that is gradually being heated is most apt. The problem is that many of the trends changing the game are slow to reveal themselves. It takes time to work out whether they have sustainable momentum in the sense that they will not disappear and they will have long-term consequences; or whether they are unsustainable in their momentum, they may actually reverse or they may lead to the exact opposite of what is expected out of them – perhaps in a sudden and vicious fashion. Personally, I would put ageing of the world's population in the first category and the lowest interest rates in modern history in the second category, but more on both later on.

Nevertheless, we know it is common sense to look in advance at sensible ways to react to a change of circumstance, albeit of the accidental and catastrophic variety. We know that preparation is a good thing and one of the keys to preparation is to select the best flags to watch out for. Even though some catastrophes come out of the blue like the terrible tsunami in December 2004, there was a flag of an abnormal withdrawal of the tide before the big wave hit. This was picked up by some humans, who knew about this kind of thing, and animals, which just sensed it. They made it to higher ground in time. The vast majority had no idea and perished in the aftermath. However, we do learn from experience and a general tsunami alert is in place, which can be activated after any earthquake under the ocean bed. The flag has already been invoked once or twice.

We also know about those places on the planet's land surface that may be prone to earthquakes because of shifting plates in the mantle. In Japan and California, for example, buildings are specially constructed to withstand severe tremors. Sadly, poverty has made this impossible in Nepal and other third world countries in earthquake zones. Yet, despite the terrible damage wrought by some events, seismologists have not discovered any flags to give you an immediate warning of this type of catastrophe. It hangs in the air and all you can do is take precautions to lower the risk.

Flagwatching can be a tricky experience, as the flooding of Brisbane in January 2011 showed. The Wivenhoe Dam was built on the Brisbane River in 1984 as a direct response to the record floods 10 years earlier in 1974. It was kept partially empty so that it could act as a buffer to unusual flows in the future. But there had been a drought for 10 years prior to 2011. So when the flag indicating abnormal weather patterns and exceptional rainfall went up in December 2010, it had to be weighed against the flag of long-term drought. Should precious water gradually be released because of the exceptional rainfall flag or should it be kept to the last possible moment with the risk of creating a shockwave because of the drought flag? That was the quandary. In the event, the second option was chosen and the water had to be released suddenly. This action seriously aggravated the surge of floodwaters into Brisbane and surrounding areas. When flags conflict with one another, it is all about good judgement and bit of luck in picking the best option.

But flagwatching is an established practice in many other sectors. Take forest or bush fires. We are given a set of flags to watch, evacuation drills to follow and designated points to assemble in the event of fire. All this is put down on paper to elicit a swift and effective response. The scenario is played and the action is specified. Options are avoided as they waste time. Changes in wind direction, however, demand the playing of scenarios and evaluation of the best options by the fire-fighting teams. Within office blocks, conference centres and other structures housing large numbers of people, safety laws demand flagwatching and drills. They are communicated in advance of any other subject being raised at a gathering inside a conference room or auditorium.

Of course, there is one crucial difference between tsunamis and earthquakes on the one hand, and fires on the other. Fires can be prevented and therefore safety includes educating people about dangerous practices which cause them and monitoring people for compliance. Prevention is as important as being the first to spot the flag when a fire happens.

Let's look at other examples of flagwatching. Subsequent to the filming incident on the railway track mentioned earlier, we did a follow-up video called *Beyond Plan B: Using your radar to navigate the future*. We shot one of the scenes in an aircraft simulator to show how pilots are trained to recognise warning lights, irregular aircraft flight behaviour and hazardous weather conditions to the point that their reflexes to rescue the situation become instinctive. Time is of the essence at 35 000 feet. Regrettably, it would appear from the recent crash of a German passenger airliner in the Alps that there is no radar system in place for a company to detect suicidal tendencies in one of its pilots. One hopes this is rectified as soon as possible across all airlines. The scenario was obviously unimaginable beforehand.

Lawyers employ historic flags to fight a case in court where two scenarios are in play – innocent or guilty. In criminal cases, the second scenario must carry a probability of more than 95% so that it is considered to be beyond reasonable doubt. In civil cases, you can be found guilty on balance of probability which means higher than 50%. The bar is set much higher for the past than for the future for good reason. It is easier to work out an account of what happened than a story envisioning what will happen. Sometimes, neither side has enough retrospective flags in their case documentation to convince a judge or jury one way or the other. Witnesses can prove to be unreliable flags under cross-examination. Then the result is no verdict.

I often say to audiences that the future can be handled like a trial where the two scenarios being presented are, one, where the status quo continues and, the other, where a tipping point is about to happen. Management sits around the table and argues the toss as in court. Flags in either direction are raised and debated and consensus is finally reached – or the CEO acts as the jury and decides. The judgement can still be wrong, but it has a better chance of being correct. Another useful analogy is that flags to a scenario planner are what clues are to the detective. The twists and turns of the future are like the ones in a good Agatha Christie novel. To disentangle the truth from the lies needs the same kind of thinking out of the box. Agatha's fictional detective, Hercule Poirot, and Pierre Wack had a lot in common, especially peripheral vision to scan the horizon for the unusual and extraordinary.

During a visit to her house in Devon in the early 1960s, Agatha was my bridge partner. We played against her daughter and grandson, Matthew Pritchard, whom I met on the cricket field. I always remember her quizzical expression when I made a bid, as if she was interpreting my intonation as a flag of confidence or slight hesitation. Of course, she was an expert at absorbing the behaviour of those in her company as potential material for a future novel. Suspicion of hidden motives behind any action or statement was her trump suit. She saw flags that nobody else did and then weaved a plot around them. Only at the end of the book, when the mystery was solved, did you recognise them.

Doctors use flags, called symptoms, to decide the kind of treatment the patient needs and the probability of a successful cure or otherwise. Medicine is seldom an exact science, prognoses have probabilities attached and in many cases only tests can tell you which scenario is in play. At a recent conference attended by nurses in Cape Town, one recommended a new name for the nursing profession: foxy flagwatchers!

Flags are literally raised on many popular beaches to warn bathers of the presence of sharks. Alas the number of shark attacks has risen worldwide, making the role of shark watchers essential to the safety of surfers and bathers alike. It is thought that the abnormally high temperatures in the ocean are driving sharks into the relatively cooler water inshore.

A sobering thought is when you buy and sell shares on the stock exchange. The person on the other side of the deal may well be as intelligent as you. Yet, he or she probably has exactly the opposite flags in mind in buying the shares you are selling, or selling the shares you are buying. If people all shared the same scenario and flags on the market's future, no trades would take place other than to realise cash or fulfil some other motive than capital gain.

Sometimes a flag can initially be seen as positive for an industry when in fact it turns out to be negative and vice versa. The finest example came out of a session I did for a motor insurance company. To begin with, they welcomed vehicle telematics where automatic driver assistance systems make the driving experience safer – like controlling the distance between you and the vehicle in front of you and robotically engaging the brakes in an emergency situation. It lowered the chances of expensive accidents on which the company had to pay out claims. Then many customers dropped the idea of insuring their vehicle comprehensively for simpler coverage at a reduced premium because they no longer felt the need to insure against all risks. Suddenly, telematics was perceived as a new technology shrinking the insurance game; and ultimately who is there to insure when you have driverless cars?

Closer to home, the expression on the face of your spouse or partner is a critical flag. Ignore it at your peril. Whether your remark is greeted by a smile or a frown will determine your next move. You watch and you decide. Flagwatching is part of our daily lives, whether we are conducting a conversation with a loved one, driving a car, being interviewed by our boss, doing a business deal or checking out the weather before going for a walk. As we all know, the fullness or emptiness of a restaurant can be a flag for the quality of the food served from the restaurant's kitchen.

So all I am proposing is that you take something which is part of your daily routine and formalise it as part of the strategic thinking process inside your company. Seek to capture the flags that are changing your business game and then decide what you are going to do about it. Look out before you look in. And remember that, as a species, we are vulnerable to overlooking the flags that slowly change the game.

Connecting flags to scenarios

As I indicated earlier on, Chantell's first point in her thesis was that scenario planning was too abstract for entrepreneurs in the real business world. Ancient Greeks had similar frustrations about the oracle of Apollo at Delphi. While the oracle had great authority, the prognostications from this source were seen to be highly ambivalent. A range of scenarios was offered which guaranteed that the oracle could never be wrong. The information was void through vagueness. It was a case of 'what ifs' from the oracle, receiving a shrug of the shoulders from the listener.

Hence, the challenge is how one can be more precise about the future without being too precise. The first step Chantell and I took was to add the idea of flags to the scenarios. In a physical universe, if a scenario is regarded as a pathway into the future, the flag is a signpost that you are possibly heading in that direction. Not definitely, but possibly; and as the flag is raised, the possibility can be turned into a probability and on rare occasions into a near certainty.

As you will see later on in the book, we are prepared to allocate percentage probabilities to the scenarios on the understanding that it is not a mathematical percentage. It is our best intuitive shot at a percentage based on our perception of how far the flag or flags relating to a scenario have gone up. We are quite prepared for people to disagree with us on the height of the flags on the flagpole and our choice of flags. But we feel the debate enriches all the participants' knowledge of not only what could happen but also the relative likelihood of it happening. Furthermore, since our clients make the final decision on changes to the strategic direction of their organisation, it is their judgement on probabilities that counts in the end.

That brings me back to Pierre Wack and his anxiety about scenario planners getting involved in the formulation of options and in making decisions. If Pierre were alive today (he died in 1997), I would try and allay his anxiety by saying that we do not trespass on management's territory as facilitators. We are actually assisting the decision makers to become scenario planners, albeit with the addition of flags to make the process more practical and down to earth. In that sense, we have reversed the flow because we do not think it is an intrusion for managers to go upstream into the construction of scenarios. It is educational and opens their minds. I know there is an argument that such a move creates the temptation to equivocate on future strategy, but my counterpunch is that it creates a much better awareness of risks to the business. Decisions still have to be made but they are based on a better judgement of potential profits and losses.

The foxy switch

Up to this point in the book, I hope that I have offered you an informative and entertaining account of how I started in the field of scenario planning, the lessons I learnt from the legendary Pierre Wack and the way Chantell Ilbury and I have developed the process into a more accessible business tool.

Now it is time to break new ground. One of the things that has struck me in many of the sessions I conduct is that participants in a strategic workshop and the audience at a conference seem to be far more interested in the flags than the scenarios. As one banker remarked in a fairly dismissive way: "Scenarios are where the rubber meets the sky!"

But it was a young man called Michael, born in Russia, raised in America and now living in South Africa, who gave me the best reason at a function at Sun City not so long ago.

He said: "The thing about flags is that they flutter in the wind and are part of our past and present. You can feel them changing the game and creating a new normal. A scenario is a hypothetical future which only becomes visible at a later date on condition that you have played the right one. The wrong ones never appear because the future has shunned them. They are quickly forgotten and dumped into the waste paper basket."

The brevity and simplicity of the statement only made it more powerful.

Ping! Being a bushy-tailed fox, I said to myself: "Why not change the order around and begin with the flags instead of identifying them as an afterthought to the scenarios? Why not bow to public demand and concentrate one's energy on identifying the game-changing flags first and then, if necessary, play scenarios around them?"

Of course, flags of interest when studying the future can come in all shapes and sizes like the national flags of countries. They can be ones changing the global game or a particular country/region. They can relate to the industry which you are in or even to the internal organisation of your company. Any flag changing any aspect of your game should be considered, whatever its scope. It can fall into numerous different categories depending on its source: a political upheaval; an economic turning point; a change in legislation, lifestyle or consumer tastes; a new technology; a shift in values as to what is moral and immoral; a new entrant to the market with a fresh approach or a revolution in product design.

It can be a trend that has just popped up or, as you will see, one extending over centuries. It can be an event or chain of events. The flag can rise so high that it goes into the stratosphere, the consequences of which are way beyond anybody's expectations. Think of the flag of the mobility of wealth of the super-rich and what it has done to London house prices. The house next door to the one in which my mother was brought up in Campden Hill, Kensington, was sold the other day for £70 million or R1.4 billion. That is what you pay for a private residence in a nice suburb in Britain's capital city, largely through foreign demand.

On the downside, think of what fracking and America's growing self-sufficiency in oil has done to the oil price. It went below $50 a barrel when the most pessimistic experts were forecasting a floor of $80. As a somewhat humbling third alternative, it can be a flag that goes up, signifying an apparent change in things to come, and then it goes down, leaving things as they are. Most people predicted ebooks would displace paperbacks as a result of the Kindle, but hardbacks and paperbacks have made a comeback. The two formats live side by side.

The bottom line is that professional flagwatchers have to keep their eyes on the flags they've chosen night and day, week in, week out. The other side of the coin is that flags are a wonderful way of screening the billions of bytes of information assaulting our senses on a daily basis. Whether you are opening a newspaper, absorbing the news on television or radio or clicking into a news website to check a developing story, you know what to look for when you have a select number of flags up your sleeve. You can disregard the rest of the content or read it for entertainment.

One final point in this section is that a flag can sometimes be identified before it has gone up at all. As mentioned earlier in the book, Chantell and I did that in *Games Foxes Play* when we chose a fall in property values as a trigger for a recession. That was in 2005 and property prices started falling in early 2007. The recession kicked in later that year.

You might say that choosing flags in advance defeats the object of flags which is to spot changes taking place right now in front of your eyes. 'What-if' flags belong to the future, not the present. My response is that I am not ruling out the painting of a scenario first – in this case the end of the boom – and then looking at what could cause it. In breaking new ground, there is still plenty of validity in our original approach and companies will still have the option of using it if it is their preference. Incidentally, the flags preceding 9/11 were already in play when we spotted them.

Events, trends and scenarios

Before we get into the real art of flagwatching, I want to do two things: more closely define three words I have been using freely and often in the text so far; and divide flags into two fundamental types in the next section. We will begin with events, trends and scenarios.

Events are the discrete moments in the stream of consciousness which we call everyday life. By their very nature, they have a definite beginning and a definite end. Nevertheless, while their period is finite, they can vary in length. An event can last a millisecond, an hour, a day, a week or even longer – from a moment in a race at the Olympics when a runner trips, to the race itself from start to finish, to the Olympics as a whole. Events are the building blocks of our experience in this world whether we are talking sight, sound or touch.

When we connect events in our sensory perceptions into a group, because they are similar and familiar, we recognise a person like our parents, we get a house like our home, a toy like a rattle (or nowadays Daddy's iPhone) and a pet like a dog we see each day. Broadly speaking, we construct our concept of living things and physical objects from the raw data we receive every waking moment. Then we start associating these concepts as with mother and food, bed and sleep, naughtiness with smacks or time out in the bathroom. As our mind shifts into second gear, we begin to understand love, hatred, comfort and fear. These are also paired with people, animals and objects.

As such, we finally gain a grasp of causality. If this happens, something else will follow. We begin to see an underlying pattern to our perceptions of the external world. At school we learn science, which is all about causality, in chemistry, physics and biology. The connection between one event and another is so predictable that it becomes a law. I am talking at the macro level rather than the micro level of atoms and electrons where the principle of uncertainty applies. The laws of science are refined over time, as experiments make more data available permitting fresh interpretations of the causal connection.

Alongside mathematics and science, we enter the world of human affairs by studying history. Initially, it is all about the dates of events but then we start stringing them together. That is when the world becomes a hazier place. Causal connections are more theoretical and can be debated. The rise and fall of nations, the outbreak of war, the ambitions and disappointments of individuals, victory and defeat in battle – they can be hotly contested as to their cause and subsequent effect. The chain of all political, economic and social developments is open to interpretation depending on which side you're on.

And so we move on to trends which are an artificial construct arising out of our perceptions of the same or similar events repeating themselves again and again. You recognise a fashion trend by looking at the sales figures of a particular brand, which constitute the same act of purchase by different people in a whole variety of locations. If sales are increasing, the trend is upwards and if sales are decreasing, the trend is downwards and another brand is replacing it. Underpinning this type of trend is a set of figures signalling growth or decline. If properly collected, they are the evidence proving the trend one way or the other.

This quantitative principle stretches across virtually any field you care to name, be it crime, sport, music, books, voting patterns, eating habits. Collect the statistics and you will get the answer. Explanations may be offered up but they are subsidiary to the figures. Equally, in the age of social media, feedback loops may mean that popularity and publicity are boosting the figures associated with a trend. We actually talk about what is trending on Twitter. But there again a trend must have initially had a life of its own to get into the public domain and be commented on.

Now we come back to the point made two paragraphs ago. Political, military, economic and social trends which provide the general material for historians to mull over tend to be much more difficult to analyse. Statistics are harder to obtain and, even where they exist, you wonder whether they've been cooked. The causal interpretation of the trends becomes even more ambiguous and I reiterate what I said earlier about courts of law. In many ways, a history book is scenario planning in reverse offering a retrospective narrative, or theme, of why things happened the way they did. And that narrative is often challenged even though it is about facts that have come and gone.

This appropriately brings us to scenarios, the third term we must unpack. They are stories of possible trends into the future. What if this or that were to happen? What is the sequence of events going forward? But now comes the crunch. How do you tell if an existing trend is going to continue into the future or if it is going to be replaced by a new one? It reminds me of the trading guru, who when asked whether the stock market was in a bubble, retorted: "You only know a bubble is a bubble when it bursts!"

My response is different. A good futurist will make the judgement call on the validity of scenarios by scrutinising the data for and against them. That data I call flags. The latter can be one-off game-changing events like Russia's annexation of Crimea. They can be long-term trends whose strength is underestimated because they are so slow that they conceal themselves from the normal view. Such a trend is the changing demographics of the world. Its momentum ensures it will continue to apply.

Flags can also be newly emerging trends which have gone largely undetected because people are totally stuck in the old groove. How many schools have adjusted their curriculum for the changing nature of employment when they are supposed to educate pupils for the job market that exists today rather than the one that existed 50 years ago?

Some scenario planners like to use the term 'driving forces' instead of flags. I have no problem with that as long as the term covers those forces with fairly precise consequences as well as those where the consequences are unclear and variable. I just prefer the word 'flag' because it is a sign of things to come. Economists use the term 'leading indicators' and I have even heard one of them use the phrase 'smoke signals' which reminds me of the Wild West comics I read in my youth. They all mean the same thing.

Clockwork and cloudy flags

Now we turn to the wisdom of the great Austrian-British philosopher Karl Popper, who dominated 20th Century philosophy in many different spheres. His one great contribution to science was to say that no scientific statement had validity unless it could be proven to be false.

There is something delightfully perverse about his notion that falsifiability was far more critical than verification in pursuing the truth. But it does, in a less stringent way, apply to the work of all scenario planners. If you read a set of scenarios produced by an individual and it strikes you as being utterly Delphic, in the sense that no actual future can contradict the overall picture painted because all possibilities are covered, then the work is of no value whatsoever.

A full 360-degree perspective does not pass the Popper test. Consequently, some futures have to be excluded by a futurist, which may actually materialise and prove him or her wrong. In technical terms, the cone of uncertainty opening up into the future has to be restricted in some way with scenarios lying outside the cone being considered highly improbable or impossible. Mind you, you cannot be too blinkered either, so it is all about balance.

However, I want to mention another of Popper's ideas which expands the frontiers of human thinking. He divided global phenomena into two types: 'clocks' on the right and 'clouds' on the left.

Clocks can be analysed into their moving parts. Moreover, the relationship that each part has with other parts, and the clock's inherent role, can clearly be demonstrated. If the clock breaks down, a clockmaker who understands the entire mechanism can repair it. For once a holistic view counts! A good clock keeps good time and seldom stops, so it is utterly predictable where the big and small hands will be at any time in the future. A Rolls Royce qualifies as a clock. Cheaper vehicles may fall into the category of clouds, to the consternation of their owners who have fallen for the advertisements promoting them as clocks.

Clouds, on the other hand, have a randomness about them that makes any prediction about them almost impossible. Think of how a cloud in a blue sky changes its shape during the day. By nature, it is ephemeral. Think of a swarm of gnats or a flock of small birds flitting around. You have little idea of where, as a group, they are going to go next and even less idea of the future position of an individual gnat or bird in the group.

Just as the hedgehog/fox analogy has proved a fruitful one for developing our ideas on scenario thinking, the clockwork/cloud analogy really helps in distinguishing the flags. A clockwork flag ticks away in the background as a fairly predictable trend that is going to continue. As you will see in the second part of the book on global flags, both climate change and demographic trends feature as clockworks flags.

By comparison, the current religious conflicts in the wake of 9/11 in the Middle East and the spate of lone-wolf terrorist attacks elsewhere are cloudy flags as nobody knows where they are going to happen next and what the consequence will be in five to 10 years' time. Russia's annexation of Crimea is a cloudy flag too, as no one knows what the end game in the military or economic arena is as a result of this action. The current condition of virtually zero interest rates in the US, Europe and Japan is a cloudy flag because of the extraordinary events that could be unleashed if the interest rate ever returns to historical norms.

So what separates clockwork from cloudy flags is that the former pretty much have one single outcome. I use the words 'pretty much' in light of the fact that the level of certainty in the real world, and particularly in that of human affairs, can never mimic that which pertains to macro science and mathematics. Cloudy flags have a range of outcomes which constantly have to be reviewed. Even then a black swan outcome, which was completely unanticipated, is possible.

An alternative foxy matrix

Not for one moment is this section about discouraging anybody from using the original foxy matrix that Chantell and I designed and which was shown earlier in the book. It has faithfully served its purpose in assisting thousands of individuals, companies and organisations facing critical moments in their existence to re-chart their future. Long may it continue to do so.

All I have done is to adapt it to reveal how clockwork and cloudy flags work in practice when one is having a conversation about them. The revised diagram, on the next page, amplifies our understanding of strategy which is still about looking out, to comprehend the changes in the environment, and then looking in, to decide what to do about it – as a fox does instinctively. The risks surrounding change are thereby exposed and better managed.

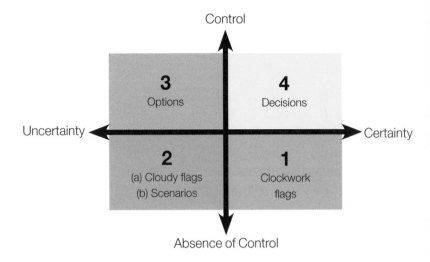

According to the revised model of flagwatching, the first thing to debate is the clockwork flags that are changing your game. These can extend from the global trends that are fairly decisive and as old as the hills to ones as young as the current year. One must acknowledge that newer trends are less trustworthy than old trends, which have been around a long time. But, in the end, it is a matter of conviction around the forward momentum of the trend, represented by the flag, as to whether it constitutes a clockwork flag or not.

After discussing the global 'whoppers' as one Australian put it, we narrow the frame of reference down to the clockwork flags affecting the country in which your business is based and the industry in which you participate. A good example is the way the internet is changing the reason people buy newspapers and the role of a bank branch in supplying services to its customers. As important, there may be the odd flag changing the internal nature of your company as well, although spotting it requires a healthy amount of introspection. I have done work with family concerns where the founder is about to retire or, worse still, fall off the perch and the rest of the team are blithely unaware of the implications. The flag is inevitable but ignored. No succession planning is done. But occasionally you have an exception. In one business I assisted, the founder, Brian, was 83 years old and had no thought of moving on. At the strategic workshop I facilitated, a young executive in his team bravely nominated his departure as a clockwork flag. So, in homage to a Monty Python movie, I wrote 'Life of Brian' with an exclamation mark on the flip chart.

Clockwork flags are a subset of the rules of the game in the original matrix. In *Games Foxes Play*, we talked of the DNA of the rules, being the descriptive rules of forces beyond your control that definitely change your game; the normative rules, which place ethical limits on your conduct; and the aspirational rules, which provide a formula for winning the game. Clockwork flags fall into the first category.

A single event rarely qualifies as a clockwork flag since the predictability of consequences flowing from it is too poor. You might wish to nominate a declaration of war as a clockwork flag and cite the examples of both world wars in the last century which utterly transformed human existence while they were being fought and for a long time after peace was restored. You might even say the legacy lives on today in institutions like the European Union which lower the risk of a repeat of 1914 and 1939. Yet, nobody knew in advance how the wars would evolve, how long they would last and, crucially, who would win them. Yes, they knew when they heard the public broadcast declaring war that the flag had ascended the pole and their lives would be completely transformed, but not how. Every war has a different dynamic about it.

As Pierre Wack advanced in years, he became more interested in isolating the predetermined elements of the specific universe he was studying. That was why he was so frustrated by the gold market. It had so few predetermined elements, or clockwork flags as I would call them, shaping its future.

He longed to compress the cone of uncertainty opening up into the future by excluding scenarios struck off the list by his predetermined elements. I used to have fun with him by postulating scenarios that might contradict one of his predetermined elements. Now I wonder whether I am suffering the same affliction on account of my love affair with flags. Maybe it is predetermined that a silver fox harbours secret ambitions to be more of a seer!

Cloudy flags are equivalent to the key uncertainties which featured in the previous model. They can be trends which have not yet consolidated into a definite pattern or path; or they can be one-off events which act as a harbinger that the playing field has moved to a new venue, maybe motivating a player to contemplate changing to a new game altogether. I am frequently asked how to spot a cloudy game-changing flag. Alas it is like trends and bubbles. You know you are in the presence of one until you are proved wrong. By their very nature, less confidence can be attached to the cloudy flags (and whether they will stay or disappear) than the clockwork flags.

One thing is certain, though: you have to play scenarios around cloudy flags and add sub-flags to indicate whether you are about to experience the best case, worst case or intermediate scenario attached to the cloudy flag. You then keep an eye on the sub-flags as a signal for the likelihood of each of the three scenarios and adjust your behaviour accordingly. One query I get is whether a cloudy flag can ever turn into a clockwork flag. The answer is yes if one of the scenarios arising from a cloudy flag gains such momentum that its probability increases to close to unity. Then that scenario becomes a predetermined trend which, as I said previously, is equivalent to being a clockwork flag.

The last three steps in the old and new matrix are exactly the same. Firstly, you look at possible futures for the organisation itself by fleshing out scenarios and giving them catchy names and themes. Then you consider your strategic and tactical options in light of the flags and scenarios; and finally you decide what you are going to do to implement the most sensible and attractive options.

The new model in action

Normally in workshops I facilitate around the new model, I divide the participants into groups of ten or fewer and ask them to come to their conclusions on the clockwork and cloudy flags at separate tables. As Peter Schwartz said: " Scenario-making is intensely participatory or it fails." It is the same with flag identification. I allow at least an hour for debate around the tables over the two types of flag. Where disagreement exists over whether a flag constitutes a definite trend or not, I ask the team to give it a rating of zero to 10 where zero is cloudy and 10 is clockwork. At the same time, I allocate a flip chart and pens to each group to write down their flags in both categories and ask them to nominate a presenter to report back on their findings in a subsequent plenary session. Comments are encouraged from the entire audience to each individual presentation. Where necessary, scenarios around the cloudy flags, prioritised by the participants, can be formulated in the open forum. I also have no problem when the different groups come up with identical flags. I ask for them to be repeated to reinforce their significance.

Then the workshop splits again into groups to formulate short- or long-term scenarios focused on the organisation under review. Our Business Gameboard is sometimes used in corporate strategy sessions as the most suitable tool to examine possible futures for the company and perhaps its individual business units. However, in other circumstances where the entity is a non-profit body or political unit, the groups may devise a completely new matrix to indicate the range of its pathways going forward.

For example, in a recent workshop I facilitated in Adelaide on the future of South Australia to 2040, the general consensus from all the groups was that the two key variables for the state were economic growth and development on the one hand and quality of life, including environmental health, on the other. These two factors then constituted the vertical and horizontal axes of the matrix with their presence or absence generating four possible scenarios. The first one was a genteel decline as the population aged in a stagnant economy but managed to retain some vestige of respectable living; the second was the boiled frog syndrome of an unexpected collapse in the economy impacting negatively on the wellbeing of all the state's inhabitants; the third was an economy growing as a result of a few big projects which made a few people insanely rich but otherwise had no significant impact on the state's high unemployment rate; and the fourth and best scenario was a vibrant economy attracting entrepreneurs from the rest of Australia and Asia because the state, and in particular Adelaide, was the most exciting place for young people to be in the country. The standard of living of all communities in South Australia was uplifted.

Returning to the new model in action and as part of the second step, I request the groups to attach the relevant flags to each scenario contained in the four quadrants of the matrix. These can be the clockwork and cloudy ones already identified in the opening session where they are applicable; but the groups can also come up with additional flags which are specific to each scenario as well. The more the flags can be converted into measurable parameters capable of some form of quantification, the easier it is to assign intuitive probabilities now and in the future to the different scenarios. We then have another plenary session to debate the scenarios and agree which are the best ones to use, the flags to watch and the current probabilities that apply to the scenarios.

Then the workshop divides for a third time into groups to discuss the options to steer the organisation towards the virtuous scenarios and away from the negative ones. Similar to the opening conversation on flags, there are two columns to consider: strategic options and tactical options. The first covers the scope of the business, including product range, product chain, geographical footprint and market segment. The second covers the running of the business including productivity schemes, remuneration structures, marketing the brand, software systems, website management, the use of social media, and how much should be done in house against being contracted out. The shape of the organisation and appropriate skills training programmes to cope with the challenges posed by the flags and scenarios can also be debated here.

A third report back to the meeting as a whole takes place and then we come to the part which focuses the collective mind on practical delivery: decisions. The groups reconvene for a last time to work out who is going to do what by when to get the show on the road in regard to the most favoured options. A final open session follows to agree on the timetable, and manner in which the decisions are to be executed. At this stage, I usually pass the baton to the CEO or the most senior person at the meeting to lay down the precise way forward after the meeting is over and provide a motivational closure. A record of the entire meeting based on the notes taken is then circulated by email with dates when progress is to be reviewed incorporated into the note. Otherwise, the entire exercise adds little if no value.

A workshop can last one or two days depending on the level of detail required and the number of business units under consideration. Where a workshop consists of fewer than ten people because it is, say, the executive committee of a company, the model remains the same but one can dispense with the report backs as they are now superfluous. The conversation can be handled in a continuous format apart from the normal breaks for tea and lunch.

One overall conclusion I have come to is this: The more participative the discussion, the greater the chance the team will become professional flagwatchers. As the future unfolds, someone will spot a new flag emanating from a change in the environment, nearby or far away. That new object on the radar screen can then be subjected to the same kind of analysis I have just described and decisions taken to stay one step ahead of your competitors or perhaps streets ahead. One company has 'a flag of the month' to encourage staff to keep their eyes peeled and one has even renamed its market intelligence function 'flagwatching'.

In summary, foxes lead the pack wherever the path may lead into the future. They are the natural flag-bearers. Hedgehogs, on the other hand, curl up in their burrows, especially when the path deviates from their vision.

Chapter 2

The global flags

Having gone through the model, it is now time to give examples of the flags themselves. I would like to repeat that the choice has nothing to do with gazing into the future using a crystal ball. Fortune tellers, palm readers and astrologers have no place in this book. We are dealing with flags that are anchored in the present and changing the world as we speak.

The only special skill needed is to distinguish between the trends and events that are game-changers and those that are not. There is no special formula for this. It is a skill acquired through trial and error, like a photographer taking snapshots. You choose the object (in this case the flag), adjust the lens, take the picture and evaluate the result. As such, flagwatching is about constantly being on the alert for a new photo opportunity and a new flag popping up. If it does, snap the flag. Then watch its progress intently by assessing all the news around it to see how it develops. Then constantly review your response to it and act accordingly. Sometimes, discard a flag as it is no longer relevant. By following this routine, flagwatching reduces the risks and maybe increases the rewards of your business and in your life.

All the flags I describe come from workshops with international and local clients. They are generic in nature as Chantell and I obviously have had to respect the confidentiality of the discussions we facilitate. I therefore cannot reveal specific flags affecting any individual client's business.

Moreover, some of the flags are interconnected where the rise of one can cause the rise of another. The list you are about to read can therefore be thought of as a web or lattice of flags. One person keen on networking imaginatively described the list as a 'flagwork'. For example, you will see further on in the book a flag covering the enormous increase in migrants and refugees flowing across borders into the more advanced economies. This is linked to the flag around religious conflict and increasing economic inequality in the world; but in future it could also be linked to the climate-change flag if people are forced to migrate from islands in the Pacific and Indian Oceans whose territory is disappearing as a result of rising sea levels. We could be faced with a combination of religious, economic and climate-change migrants or refugees.

On the other hand, the rise of one flag can cause the lowering of another. The grey flag representing the ageing of Europe's population could be offset by the wave of refugees to which I have referred in the previous paragraph. Hence, the flagwork has to be examined as an entire system to make sense of the future.

The religious flag

Sadly, this flag is at the top of the flagpole and unfurled to its full length in the wind. It is a very cloudy flag.

I mentioned how we had raised it before 9/11 in the letter to President Bush in *The Mind of a Fox*. I would like now to quote an excerpt from the introduction published in the book's second impression in the immediate aftermath of the tragedy: "The natural temptation for the rich old millions in the West must be to batten down the hatches and isolate themselves in a Gilded Cage. We all know that security is the most basic of all human needs. However, this could lead to an even more divided world as the gap between the rich old millions and the poor young billions widens further. The increasing tension and stress associated with this scenario will ironically make it more likely than before that another evil act of the same – or perhaps even greater – magnitude will be perpetrated by terrorists. No advances in technology, no improvements in intelligence and security management systems can render an individual nation impregnable against attack. The terrorist will always find a chink in the bars of the cage, however thick you make them, to pass through and commit his foul deed. Moreover, the knowledge of how to manufacture weapons of mass destruction is itself indestructible. And it will continue to spread. Meanwhile, inside the cage, a superabundance of soft targets awaits the terrorists. The growing interdependencies and networks of a modern society make it increasingly vulnerable to dislocation and attack, particularly by people who are prepared to die in the process. The only way to minimise – not entirely eliminate – the threat of further outrages is for America to take the lead in building a Friendly Planet. This involves more than a military victory over the terrorists. The realisation has to dawn that to be a secure winner, you cannot be surrounded by resentful losers."

I would not alter one word in light of all the terrorist attacks since 9/11, even though we have not had another 9/11 type event. What has happened is that the threat has profoundly changed. In an article entitled "God's Messy War" which I wrote for *News24* in May 2013, I said the following: "The Boston bombings indicate that self-radicalisation – a term to denote an individual's conversion from religious zealotry to acts of violence – is on the increase. From an intelligence point of view, this turn of events is potentially very dangerous as it is impossible to pick up the signs of a specific individual taking the leap from abstract idea to ghastly deed; and the measures required to reduce the probability of this scenario become extremely costly in terms of money and denial of freedoms which are the foundation of democracy."

The incidents in Sydney, London, Paris, Toronto and Chattanooga, Tennessee, as well as the recent killing of 38 tourists on a Tunisian beach emphasise this new development.

7/7 in London

Recently Britain commemorated the 10th anniversary of the terrible Tube and bus bombings on 7th July 2005. The civilian death toll was 52 while 700 people sustained minor to hideous injuries. I was in London at the time because Chantell and I had just jointly facilitated a strategy session in Scotland for one of Britain's largest companies. I had returned from Glasgow the previous evening and our client accommodated me at a hotel overlooking the Thames near Westminster. I went for a long walk to Kensington Gardens the following morning and thought I would get a taxi home. There was none available and I walked all the way back to the hotel, totally unaware of what was going on.

When I arrived at the hotel, I asked the receptionist whether Ken Livingstone's congestion charge had in any way affected the supply/demand situation for taxis. She replied that there had been an abnormal power surge in the Tube system and people were using taxis to get to work. I thought, "That's odd," and went up to my room and turned on the television. The first thing I saw was the bus in Tavistock Square with its roof blown off and then I knew this was a terrorist attack. I had promised to go and see my mother, who was living in a retirement home near Salisbury in Wiltshire, that afternoon. The TV reporter said that the mainline stations were opening at 2pm while the Tube would remain closed for the rest of the day.

I decided there and then to pack my bags and walk to Waterloo Station via Westminster Bridge. When I got to the centre of the bridge, I looked both ways and I was the only object of any kind on the bridge. I wondered if there had ever been another moment in the life of the bridge when it was holding up just one person in broad daylight. That was the level of disruption caused that day by the flag of wrath. I then proceeded to Waterloo and caught the train to Salisbury. That evening I heard the streets were packed with people trekking home after work. As Boris Johnson, London's Mayor, said on the 10th anniversary of the bombings, the spirit of Londoners lives on and it is the same great city that it always was.

Why am I including this story? The answer is twofold. Firstly, the G8 (as Russia was still a member of this exclusive club) was meeting at Gleneagles in Scotland at the time. Most of the attention of the British police and security services was focused on protecting the high and mighty leaders who had assembled for this event. On our way to Glasgow airport in a taxi on the night before the bombings, we noticed a heavy police presence, even in Glasgow. Secondly, the number seven is significant in several religions, including Islam. Combine the two flags and some intelligence agent in MI5 should have used lateral thinking to recognise that 7/7 could be a significant day in London's history. At the very least, the public should have been asked to be on special alert for suspicious behaviour.

Sunni and Shia

The religious flag has also changed in another fundamental manner. We now have a deep division within the Islamic world itself between Sunni and Shia, the first with its centre of gravity in Saudi Arabia and the second in Iran. We almost have a war by proxy between these two nations. I was a guest speaker on an American cruise ship in March 2015 and my fellow guest speaker was Egypt's former ambassador to Washington. He said that when he was brought up as a child, he never once heard the words Sunni and Shia. Now it is the principal force polarising people in the Middle East and it has turned the Arab Spring into the Arab Nightmare. Countries like Syria, Iraq and Yemen are disasters and Afghanistan is close behind. Borders are being redrawn with the Islamic State carving a new territory out of Syria and Iraq. Turkey, which

Ataturk converted into the most secular of Islamic countries, has been drawn into the war. Elsewhere Israel is still in conflict with Hamas and no progress has been made on a settlement between Israelis and Palestinians.

The religious flag has now spilled over into North Africa. Libya is a labyrinth of competing militias. Tunisia, which is held up as the brightest outcome of the Arab Spring, has shown how vulnerable it is to terrorist attack. Nigeria is split with the north versus the south, Mali is becoming a hot bed of activists and Kenya had that terrible attack on the Westgate shopping mall in Nairobi in 2013. On the other side of the world, relations between India and Pakistan remain uneasy which periodically lead to attacks like the one on the Taj hotel in Mumbai in 2008. Kashmir continues to be a disputed zone and it should be remembered that both antagonists are nuclear-armed. A district popular to tourists on the Indonesian island of Bali was the site of bombings in 2002 which left 202 people dead including 88 Australians.

The religious flag is not at the moment an existential threat to the West like the next one I am going to mention and it certainly has not resulted in anything like the number of deaths in either of the two world wars. But it has consumed an enormous amount of resources and time. It is estimated that America has spent $6 trillion on trying to sort out the Middle East since the first Iraq war. This represents a little under a third of its national debt. It is debatable whether the world is a safer place for Westerners inside or outside of their countries when it comes to further terrorist attacks. Indeed, the worst case scenarios flowing out of this cloudy flag suggest that things can get far uglier. A sub-flag for me is that terrorist groups will improve the technologies they use in carrying out their acts. In particular, I am worried about the use of drones carrying explosives with the intent of causing devastation in a crowded stadium.

Worst, best and middle case scenarios

The ultimate downside is covered in our letter to President Bush: "From your point of view, nuclear weapons landing up in the wrong hands must be at the top of the agenda. Proliferation means aggravation, and the knowledge of how to construct a nuclear device is now freely available on the internet. So it's just a matter of time before somebody really nasty gathers the money, the materials and the engineering skills necessary to manufacture it. You only need one terrorist organisation to hold the rich old millions to ransom by planting a hidden nuclear bomb in the middle of one city for everyone to realise that conventional military capability is useless against such a threat. An army can't find a needle in the haystack, let alone destroy it."

Negotiators for the major powers who have pressed Iran to drop any idea of constructing a nuclear weapon in exchange for lifting sanctions probably had this scenario in mind. We now have to wait and see whether the agreed deal is actually implemented and the parties comply with it.

One of the things I stress in the whole technique of flag-watching is that you really have to study the true nature of a flag to come up with viable options to cope with it. I do not think America and for that matter Britain has come close to doing that. For a start, their enemy is dispersed and tactics against a dispersed enemy have to be completely different to one with massed armies, fleets of ships, squadrons of aircraft and whose population is concentrated in major cities. The idea that you can bomb a dispersed enemy out of existence is ridiculous. As one Vietnam War veteran explained to me, the Vietcong won because they were nowhere to be seen for a set-piece battle. Moreover, the level of collateral damage – for that read the number of civilian casualties – was such that the untouched villages secretly supported the Vietcong and offered shelter to them. In short, the more you bomb, the more you create new recruits for your opposition.

The other critical factor is that this flag constitutes a war of beliefs and that is very different to a normal war over territorial gain or other earthly ambitions. To win this kind of war, you have to win the hearts and minds of people. The last way you do that is to make their life more miserable by flattening their country with bombs and destroying their economy. As one Californian member of the audience on the cruise ship said: "Maybe we should be investing in places like Syria so that economic prosperity takes their minds away from fundamentalist dogmas. People of different persuasions get along much better if they are creating wealth together. They eschew movements promoting death and destruction."

In London, in December 2014, one of my co-speakers at a mining conference had just retired as the deputy military head of NATO forces in Europe. He compared the success of the British campaign in Northern Ireland where the troops and the local population had a certain degree of mutual understanding for each other with the failure of the venture in Basra, Iraq, where neither had any idea of what made the other one tick. The implication is that the West has to come up with a package that goes beyond war in order to halt terrorism. It has to make a real effort to comprehend other cultures on equal terms. Only then may peace break out.

That is the best case scenario. At present, one of the likely outcomes is a middle-of-the-road scenario: The religious flag stays up for the remainder of this century because of a stalemate. Nobody wins, but nobody loses other than the local population desperately trying to lead normal lives. Each terrorist attack is followed by revenge bombings with no long-term strategy to end the war. Troops on the ground are only introduced by the West if the ferocity of the attacks becomes unbearable. The Sunnis and the Shias continue to slug it out. Like the Crusades dominated world history nearly a thousand years ago, we will suffer another drawn-out cycle of religious conflict. If Saudi Arabia, Iran or Israel is drawn directly into the war, the scenario deteriorates considerably.

Hence, God has begun to crop up in the discussions in the boardroom of many companies because the flag is affecting them commercially in so many different ways. For investors, it is changing the risk profile of the Middle East and making it harder to do business there. This also applies to countries in Africa affected by this flag. The oil industry could well feel the heat with clashes around significant wells and refineries.

Tourism, one of the biggest global industries on which millions of small businesses depend, is also taking a knock. Places where Western tourists congregate in large numbers anywhere in the world must now take extra security measures to ensure the safety of their visitors. Otherwise the latter will stop travelling overseas with massive repercussions for the developing world. At the same mining conference I mentioned a little earlier on, an expert on hostage negotiations gave an address on how companies stood the most chance of getting back any of their management and workers captured in war-torn areas by terrorists. His counsel was to pay the ransom and walk away with no thought of revenge. The point about mining is that you cannot choose the location of where you are mining now or where the next big mineral discovery will be. Ore deposits are fixed on the Earth's crust.

Complicating the whole problem is another flag around porous borders which I will feature later on. Waves of refugees are entering developed countries in Europe and elsewhere legally and illegally. This is not only changing the religious complexion of existing society in these countries; it is also feared that among the large numbers of refugees may be potential 'lone wolves' planted by the terrorist groups. Sleeper cells of home-grown extremists with plenty of time to conceive new plots are now a well-established phenomenon. I am afraid that intelligence gathering is one of the games that has to be enhanced massively to handle the consequences of the religious flag. Meanwhile, the ideal of converting the Middle East into a series of secular democracies run on Western lines may have to be put on hold for the rest of this century.

The red flag

This flag is an existential threat to the West and it is very red indeed. It is about Russia or, more specifically Vladimir Putin, and it went up with the annexation of Crimea in 2014. Overnight the prospects for Europe were changed. Would you believe that only five years ago there was talk in certain quarters of Russia joining the European Union? That has been taken off the table completely. Now we are up to the third level of sanctions between America and Europe on the one hand and Russia on the other with the prospect that they could be escalated further.

America is leading the charge against Russia because it has nothing to lose in economic terms. Its total exports only constitute 10% of its GDP and a fraction of those go to Russia. Americans basically buy and sell from each other. Moreover, fracking will make it self-sufficient in energy and, other than platinum, Russia has virtually no product of note to make America wince by withdrawing it from the market. In short, Americans couldn't care less about Russia's economic condition.

Europe is a different kettle of fish. Each country generally exports a much higher percentage of its GDP than America, of which a large part goes to other member countries of the European Union but also to Russia. Moreover, Russia provides Europe with at least a quarter of its energy needs in terms of gas and oil. Half of that is pumped through Ukraine. But the most worrying feature of all is that Germany – Europe's star economy – is Russia's closest trading partner and has extensive business interests inside Russia itself. Angela Merkel speaks fluent Russian and, lest one forget, it was not so long ago that East Germany was part of the Soviet Union. Major economic ties still exist between the two countries.

In the tit-for-tat game of sanctions, Europe's fragile economic recovery can be dealt a serious blow. Farmers have already blockaded the streets of Brussels to obtain compensation for their loss of income due to Russia banning food imports from its Western neighbours. Russia will suffer too; but Russians, as history shows, have generally got a much higher tolerance for hardship than Europeans, who potentially have a lot more to lose. Meanwhile, Putin is riding a huge wave of popularity in his home country by restoring national pride and putting Russia on the map again. His approval rating is currently 80% which, even allowing for some exaggeration, puts him way ahead of Barack Obama or any European leader. Some people see parallels to Germany in the 1930s when Adolf Hitler took advantage of the economic misery caused by the Treaty of Versailles, followed by hyperinflation and on its heels the Depression.

The Russian economy has sagged while the rouble has fallen appreciably against the US dollar and other world currencies. Russians are just as angry today with their lot as the Germans were in the 1930s and, like the Germans, are blaming it on external forces. An interesting historical note is that during the Roaring Twenties, the Americans had no idea of the pressures building up in Germany that ultimately produced Hitler and the re-militarisation of Germany. The Charleston was far more important. Could you see a repeat? It requires a close study of the red flag to judge the possibility.

Sadly Ukraine, besides being an ethnic smorgasbord, is also an economic mess and has been ever since its independence. At least when it was in the Soviet orbit everybody had a job. Now, like Russia, society is divided between the oligarchs and the rest, many of whom are unemployed. Inequality and corruption have shot up. A civil war will only worsen the situation.

Meanwhile, China remains neutral because it does not want to anger the Russians with whom it shares a border. Moreover, they were allies during the Korean War and shared the ideology of Communism until the late 1980s. On the other hand, it needs access to America's market to grow its economy. Walking on egg shells is probably the appropriate term for China's diplomatic strategy on the Ukrainian issue.

Like the first flag, the red flag is also a very cloudy one, around which you can play multiple scenarios. While some of our major German clients are extremely concerned about it for all the reasons quoted above, the buoyancy of the German Stock Exchange – always a good indication of crowd forecasting in Germany – implies that the risks are small. I back our clients against the market on this one, the reason being that the military scenarios are a lot worse than the economic ones. Furthermore, wars are something the public doesn't entertain as a possibility until they actually happen. With hindsight, historians show how the conflict was inevitable. All this has nothing to do with Germany and everything to do with the rivalry that created the Cold War.

Russians and Americans

We are talking about the relationship between Russia and America. In 1984, one of my favourite recording artists was Al Stewart, a British singer, who composed and sang offbeat folk songs. In that year, he produced an album on which there was a memorable song titled *Russians and Americans*. One of the verses goes as follows: "Russians and Americans driven by the past, the Third World moves in the shadows you cast. Russians and Americans could turn the world to dust, so much to live for, so much undiscussed. So much in common and so little trust." Those lyrics have lost none of their relevance.

Both nations have the richest of histories. The populations of both countries have enormous national pride. Yet, as the recent events in Ukraine and more specifically Crimea have shown, they have a deep antipathy and suspicion towards each other. They have different world views, although they agree that the global marketplace has integrated to the point that we are now a global village. The issue is how much of the village belongs in spirit to America and how much to Russia. Whenever any nation like Greece gets into trouble, they fight over whose fiefdom it should be in. Importantly, they are both armed to the teeth with nuclear weapons, which up till now has meant that neither side will want to use them for fear of counter-attack.

The last time they nearly came to blows was in October 1962 when both were considerably more powerful than they are today. Russia was the Soviet Union and America owned a much bigger chunk of the world's economy. Since then the wall has come down in Berlin, and China and Japan have ascended the economic rankings. The issue in 1962 was the Cuban missile crisis and the real risk – discovered through subsequent research – was that, at the time, each country completely misread the other's position.

As Chantell and I described it when we were writing about key uncertainties in *The Mind of a Fox*: "Despite both sides having formidable intelligence networks, each leader was given woefully incorrect information on how his counterpart was thinking. So we nearly blundered into a nuclear war. But ask yourself: How often do you make decisions based on perfect knowledge of all the facts? Admit it – the answer is seldom, if ever."

Misperception has to be the greatest risk of unleashing the dogs of war at the moment. You only have to watch the TV news channels CNN and Russia Today to realise how the narrative on events since the annexation of Crimea depends on which channel you listen to. For Russians, it was a Western-backed coup in Ukraine and they are protecting their naval interests in Crimea as well as Russian-speaking citizens there. After all, America would never hand back their military base of Diego Garcia in the Indian Ocean to the original islanders. For Americans, the current Ukranian government is perfectly legal and the Russians have invaded a sovereign state. They accuse each other of hypocrisy but America has stated that relations can never return to normal until Crimea is handed back to Ukraine.

Is the voluntary return of Crimea a likely scenario? The answer is no. Most Russians believe that Crimea is an inseparable part of Russia which was temporarily ceded to Ukraine in 1954 by Nikita Khrushchev who was then General Secretary of the Communist Party. It is now back where it belongs. Will it be returned as sanctions are gradually cranked up on Russia, leaving it no other option? Maybe; but that is where the scenarios start spreading out. Already, mission creep has slipped into Russian strategy in that they are assisting the Russian rebels in Eastern Ukraine. Can the creep extend to other countries where there are significant Russian minorities?

In a sense Ukraine is Russia's window on the West, as all the other former members of the Soviet Union on its Western border (except Belarus) have joined the European Union and are members of NATO. If Ukraine were to do the same, it would just about complete Russia's loss on its Western front. Hence, from a Russian perspective, the stakes are very high and it is unlikely that it will go into reverse on its policy – whatever the economic cost of sanctions.

That brings us to the ultimate scenario of a flat-out exchange of nuclear missiles between America and Russia.

While America outspends Russia enormously in the military sphere, the latter is a mean military machine with a nuclear arsenal rivalling, if not exceeding, that of the Americans. Ominously, Putin announced recently the addition of 40 state-of-the-art intercontinental ballistic missiles to the Russian nuclear armoury. America immediately retorted that Russia had broken the strategic arms limitation treaty. Nevertheless, Putin continuously mentions the nuclear option these days in a way that leaves US diplomats experienced in Cold War politics scratching their heads in disbelief. One said the other day that America used to have a feel for Russian logic during the Cold War; now they are totally mystified. They no longer know where nuclear weapons sit in Russia's order of battle, nor what would signal their imminent use.

Revisiting nuclear game theory

As a result of the red flag, I have for some time been calling for a review of nuclear game theory before the rivalry between Russia and America becomes unstoppable in its progress towards a nuclear showdown. Nobody wants a Third World War. I quote the following event in support of this review. On 31 October 1961, Russia detonated the most powerful nuclear weapon of all time, before or since. The site was a remote archipelago in the Arctic Ocean, north of the Russian coast. The blast was equivalent to between 50 and 58 megatons of TNT or 1 400 times the combined power of the two atom bombs dropped on Japan in August 1945.

Think of taking one step a metre long versus walking 1.4 kilometres. That is the difference. Named Tsar Bomba and nicknamed 'We'll show you', the device weighed 27 tons and measured 8x2 metres. The subsequent mushroom cloud was 64 kilometres high but, more to the point, it destroyed all buildings in a village 55 kilometres from ground zero. Dropped centrally on any major city today, it would virtually flatten it in a single blast and instantly kill between a quarter and a third of its inhabitants.

Classic game theory examines every possible strategy a player must consider when taking into account all the responses of his or her adversary. It obviously applies to nuclear conflicts as well. Now you have the two most heavily armed nations locking horns as they did in 1962, eyeball to eyeball like two chess players poring over the next move. John von Neumann, a US Hungarian mathematician, was the founder of game theory in 1928. He later coined the acronym MAD which stands for 'mutually assured destruction' in the nuclear game. The argument was that neither of the two players would resort to nuclear conflict if a first strike by either one triggered a response by the other which caused an overwhelming loss to the initial aggressor. Thus, a second strike capability on both sides guaranteed peace between them according to the principle of minimising your maximum potential loss. The latter is a core element of optimising your strategy under game theory. Put crisply, if you nuke me, I'll nuke you, so let's be sensible and not nuke each other.

In 1985 there were an estimated 68 000 active nuclear warheads around the world. As a consequence of disarmament treaties since then, the figure is now put at 4 100, with the bulk being fairly equally distributed between Russia and America.

The remainder are in the hands of the UK, France, China, India, Pakistan, North Korea and Israel. To keep the equilibrium demanded by MAD, treaties between the two nuclear players have also limited the numbers of strategic launchers, heavy bombers and anti-ballistic missile systems owned by each. However, a destabilising factor is that while 17 300 warheads are reckoned to have been decommissioned, they have yet to be destroyed.

In addition, a single intercontinental ballistic missile can deliver as many as 10 separate warheads at a time. They can be accompanied by 40 decoys so that 50 rockets are required to neutralise an incoming missile. Secrecy means outsiders have no idea of the latest technical advances in attack or defence systems. Nevertheless, one can surmise that neither side has an anti-ballistic missile system to offer complete protection for its cities. The full military option therefore has as much downside for America as it does for Russia – if not more for America since it is a much wealthier nation.

As an aside, Ukraine had around 5 000 nuclear warheads when it became independent of the Soviet Union in 1991. By 1996, all these weapons had been voluntarily sent to Russia for disassembly. I wonder how Ukraine feels about that handover now.

I have listed all these statistics to demonstrate that a worst case scenario for the red flag has to receive a thorough examination, even if it has a minimal probability of occurrence. For the world to begin an unanticipated slide into a Third World War is too awful to contemplate. A random event can start the whole plunge. I thought the shooting down of the passenger aircraft belonging to Malaysian Airlines over Ukraine in July 2014 might be such a trigger. It wasn't.

Now Russian fighter jets are regularly flying over parts of the British Isles and have to be escorted out of British airspace by the RAF. Russian submarines are seen in Swedish waters. Mr Putin is testing Western resolve. He knows that nations on the European mainland spend less than 2% of GDP on defence, the target set by NATO. Only Britain squeaks in with some clever accounting.

If John von Neumann were alive today, I would want to ask him the following questions. Maybe someone from the Institute for Advanced Study in Princeton, New Jersey, where Von Neumann was based, is sufficiently well versed in game theory to act as a substitute:

Is MAD still a valid concept which makes nuclear conflict highly improbable? Is the Doomsday scenario widely accepted? Or do military strategists now play nuclear war games where they examine less apocalyptic sequels? If so, do they look at a conventional war preceding a nuclear exchange, or the other way around?

What would be the estimated damage and loss of life caused by a nuclear conflict between the US and Europe on the one hand and Russia on the other? What harm would be done to the environment in the short and long term?

What would the impact be on the rest of the world and would the whole world recover from such a global war as quickly as it did in 1945?

What are the probabilities of the current game in Ukraine remaining localised or deteriorating into a direct military conflict between the major players with potential nuclear consequences?

Does the chance of terrorists acquiring nuclear weapons nullify MAD, since they belong to no fixed abode which can be destroyed if they attack first, and are prepared to die for their cause?

How does emotion feature in the mathematical models of game theory since patriotism as much as logic can be responsible for the onset of nuclear war?

I have not come across a single word in the printed or social media, on the internet, on television or radio or anywhere in the public domain addressing this issue. Russia has been kicked out of G8 (which is now G7) so the red flag cannot be discussed by that forum with Russia's participation. As a flag-watcher and scenario planner, you always look at the end game to decide what your next move should be. That is why Herman Kahn – the father of scenario planning – wrote his famous book *On Thermonuclear War* in 1960, followed by *Thinking about the Unthinkable* in 1962. This section is just an update on the thoughts of Kahn.

Business, especially in Germany, is meanwhile sitting on

the sidelines watching the showdown between the Russian bear and the American buffalo. Russian plutocrats do not appear to be overly anxious as they have recently bought a greater number of expensive houses in London than any other nationality including the British themselves. Presumably, they do not believe that the world is on the eve of destruction, with London about to be razed to the ground by one of their own nukes. In the end, a compromise may be reached which is classified as neither appeasement nor victory, but which, for the time being, is a solution. I would like to draw this section to a close with another line from Al Stewart's famous song: "Russians and Americans, tell me if it's true. You really believe all the things that you've said. The red-white-and-blue running into the red."

I am not sure how I would accommodate that on a flag. Maybe for once we should feel lucky as South Africans to be in the Southern Hemisphere, a long way away from the immediate area of the conflict. However, this flag could pose a tricky choice for the South African government if things go really pear-shaped. Do they support Russia as a fellow member of BRICS, the new economic grouping consisting of Brazil, Russia, India, China and South Africa, which has just established the New Development Bank headquartered in Shanghai? Do they support America because it does not help to be on the wrong side of the largest economy on Earth? Or do they choose a middle course like China? Life becomes complicated in a divided world.

The grey flag

Unlike its two predecessors, this is a clockwork flag ticking away in the background with consequences that can be anticipated. Thus there is no need to play scenarios. We are dealing with a definite trend. It is the ageing of the world's population.

Let us start with two statistics which explain the flag. In 1900, the life expectancy of newborn children in America and Britain was 46 years for a boy and 50 years for a girl. By 2000 it had risen to 74 for boys and 80 for girls. In other words, we added 60% to our lifespan as a species in 100 years. This was due to the advances in medicine and healthier living. During the same century, the human population – which hit the one billion mark in 1810 – went from 1.6 billion to 6.1 billion. It is now over seven billion as we are adding an extra billion people every 12 years.

The net result is that we not only have a lot more people sharing their existence on this planet, we have a lot more elderly people as well. In my first book, *The World and South Africa in the 1990s*, I referred to the rich old millions who lived in the developed world and the poor young billions who lived in the developing world. The former at the time of writing the book in 1987 represented 15% of the world's population and are now down to 12% on account of a much lower birth rate than that in the developing world.

The club of countries in the developed world – comprising North America, the UK and Western Europe, Japan, Australia and New Zealand – has remained virtually unchanged over the last 50 years. Other than oil countries like Qatar and tax havens like the Cayman Islands, the only countries to have entered the present club (defined by having a GDP per capita of more than $35 000 in 2014) are Singapore, Iceland, South Korea and Hong Kong if you count Hong Kong as a country. China itself, despite being the second largest economy in the world, is well outside the club at a GDP per head of $12 000.

These demographic trends have had an extraordinary impact on the global economy. In America, all the baby boomers born after the Second World War are now geriatric boomers. As I wrote in my first book in 1987: "Already there is a growing controversy about the future adequacy of state health care and pensions. Ultimately, a higher propensity to save may appear among those of working age as the state is forced to diminish its role in the provision of benefits for the elderly."

Some things change and some stay the same. Compare my words with what Robert J Samuelson said in an article in *The Washington Post* in June 2015. Its title was "Our runaway spending on the elderly". He remarked: "A recent Congressional Budget Office report 'The 2015 Long-Term Budget Outlook' reminds us that the federal government is slowly becoming an agency for taking care of the elderly. Almost everything else is being crowded out."

He maintained that at the moment social security and major health programmes consume about half the budget, a large chunk of that for the elderly. By 2040 with no revision to policy that ratio could rise to two-thirds. His recommendations encapsulate the finishing words of my quote: Spread the pain by charging higher premiums on medical aid, cutting benefits, increasing the age for eligibility, eliminating some programmes altogether and hiking taxes in general. Otherwise, given the fact that health care by the day is getting more expensive, the budget deficit will soar out of control. In my judgement, if they do not accept this sensible advice, American politicians will show the same lack of will as Greek politicians in grasping the nettle of the grey flag.

I guess you can blame the financial situation in which many countries find themselves on my great-great-aunt, Beatrice Webb. Apart from founding the London School of Economics and establishing *The New Statesman* journal with her husband Sidney, she sat on the Royal Commission on the Poor Law which met between 1905 and 1909. Her minority report is widely recognised to have laid the foundation stone for the introduction of the welfare state in Britain in the late 1940s.

From my conversations with fund managers, pension and

medical aid schemes are already running into trouble because people are living longer and the return on the schemes' investments has fallen. The reason for the latter is that the equity markets are not performing as they did in the last century and interest rates are at an all-time low. In my opinion, that is not about to change because the rising proportion of the elderly is slowing down the world economy. In addition, medical aid schemes are finding it more difficult to use younger members with fewer visits to the doctors to cross-subsidise the older members' costly hospital bills.

In the UK, the grey flag has created a crisis in the National Health Scheme. Doctors in accident and emergency units linked to state hospitals are complaining that they have nowhere to put serious accident cases after operating on them. The reason is that the wards are full of elderly people who refuse to quit their beds and go home. The only solution is to expand hospital wings and install more beds, but that costs money.

A steady state economy

Nevertheless, the nation most affected by the grey flag is Japan. It has the highest proportion of any country of elderly citizens. In September, 2014, 33% were above the age of 60, 26% above the age of 65 and 12.5% above the age of 75. A combination of lower fertility, higher life expectancy and virtually zero entry of migrants have contributed to Japan's ageing process. At the same time, the Japanese government estimates that the total population will fall from 127 million in 2015 to 95 million in 2050. It is already declining.

Pierre Wack once said to me that if you want a feel for a nation's long-term economic growth prospects, take a look at its demographics. On this basis, Japan's economic future will resemble what has happened since the great property crash of 1990. From 1992 to 2013, Japan's GDP grew annually at 0.84% in real terms, a far cry from the 9% annual growth rate achieved between 1953 and 1965 and 4 to 6% experienced during the late 1970s and 1980s. Essentially Japan has become a steady state economy in the zero to 1% per annum growth range despite all efforts to boost the economy, including negative interest rates where you pay to have your money on deposit in the bank and quantitative easing which is a euphemism for printing new money.

Pierre's hypothesis implies that never again in its history will Japan have an economy growing at a reasonable rate. Old people don't eat as much. They don't do anything as much! Thus, the Japanese economy will be flat forever, the antithesis of the growth paradigm which has been the overarching ambition of mankind since the start of the Industrial Revolution 250 years ago.

The Japanese don't really mind because they are an affluent society which is more equal than others and has a low level of unemployment. They are also great savers. The worst thing that happens to them is earthquakes which flood a nuclear power plant. Otherwise, with a flat economy and a declining population they will achieve that which is the fervent wish of all countries: rising income per head. Welcome to a new economic model for success.

Europe is not far behind the Japanese in becoming a steady state economy, although it has a higher influx of young migrants. The figures for 2014 show a slightly positive and slightly negative population growth rate depending upon which European country you choose. All countries are ageing and therefore facing the same challenge of how to balance the national budget against caring for the increasing number of elderly citizens.

In contrast, America has a relatively young population as a result of a more generous attitude towards immigration. The population increase, at 0.77% in 2014, was high by industrialised country standards. The proportion of over 65s is reckoned to be 14.5% compared to 26% in Japan. The critical age group for consumer spending – the 35 to 45 year olds – is growing healthily. All in all, judged on its demographics, America has a natural economic growth rate of 2 to 3% a year and is therefore a more resilient economy than the UK, Europe or Japan.

This is borne out in the performance of Wall Street versus the stock market in the City of London. The Dow Jones Industrial Average peaked at 11 723 in January, 2000 and is 16 300 today. That is an increase of nearly 40%. The Financial Times Stock Exchange Index 100 in the UK peaked at 6 950 in December 1999 and is just below 6 100 today. So, but for dividends, you would have made a loss there. The lesson is simple: Invest in companies located in countries with younger populations or foreign companies that do a fair amount of business with or in those countries. Stay away from companies whose customer base is limited to an ageing domestic market. The only European stock market that has come close to Wall Street is the German one where the DAX has risen 20% from its 2000 peak but that is because Germany is the world's third largest exporter after China and America.

China's bulge and Africa's youth

That brings us to the effect of the grey flag on China. China's one child policy, instituted in 1978, has slowed population growth to 0.47% in 2014 with the total population now standing at 1.376 billion. The demographics have so far had a limited impact on the economy which has slowed from a growth rate of around 10% per annum a few years ago to 7% today. The latter figure is a rate that most nations would die for but for the Chinese it has been a bit of a disappointment. One of the reasons that the economy is doing relatively well is that the 65s and over represent 9.4% of the population, which is significantly lower than America's 14.5%. However this is all about to change.

If you look at projections of China's demographics to 2030, an extraordinary thing happens. Normally, a graph showing a breakdown of population by age looks like a pyramid with the base of the pyramid representing the greater numbers of young people (males and females on either side of the vertical axis) and the top the few people of both genders who make it to more than a century. In 2030, even with a re-laxation of the one child policy, the shape of the Chinese population transforms into a middle-aged bulge around the 50 to 65 year olds with fewer numbers in the younger and older age groups. A child born in 1977, a year before the restriction on new births started, will be 53 in 2030 and that is the cause of the bulge. Later in the 2030s, China may join Japan with more people over the age of 50 than under the age of 50. That is a significant milestone and it does assume that China continues its virtual ban on immigrants becoming Chinese citizens.

The other result of China's one child policy is a skewed gender distribution in favour of men. Currently, for every 100 baby girls being born, there are 120 boys which is shifting the graph of overall population to the male side.

Consequently, should you give credibility to Pierre's hy-pothesis of linking demographics to future economic growth rates, it is almost inevitable that China is on a downward path to a steady state economy. But there is a huge difference between Japan and Europe on the one hand and China on the other. The former have reached a ceiling of relative affluence before levelling out whereas China will never get there in terms of GDP per head. As one American demographer observed to me: "China will be the first nation to grow old before it gets rich." Moreover, by 2100 the UN projects that the Chinese population will have fallen to a total of just over one billion people, losing more than the whole of America's current population in numbers during the remainder of the century.

Recently, there was a sharp reversal in China's stock market boom, which the authorities managed to stabilise through various interventions. However, one gets the feeling that China's financial system will continue to be fragile on account of the slowdown in economic growth. New apartment buildings remain unoccupied, industrial projects to increase cement and steel production have resulted in a huge oversupply of these products; and the grey banking system has financed much of the expansion without adequate safeguards. The chickens could come home to roost in a spectacular way. Another red flag is the devaluation of the yuan which has caught markets by surprise, but which the Chinese government is allowing to happen to boost exports. A currency war may ensue, leading to the Great Fall of China.

Of course, such a gloomy outlook for the second largest economy in the world has enormous implications for many industries as there is no other national economy close to China's size at the moment to replace it (I am excluding America, which is already in pole position). Higher economic rates in India, Africa, South America, South Korea and Indonesia can offset a Chinese slowdown to a certain extent but we are unlikely to return to the boom-time conditions of the latter half of the last century. The mining and energy industries will be particularly affected as China has accounted for around 80% of the growth in demand for most primary products. I have to say that no economic expert has yet contradicted Pierre's theory and my application of it to China.

Africa is the exact opposite of the grey flag. It has the youngest population in the world. The median age – which is the age that equally divides a population into two numerically equal groups, half older, half younger – of most sub-Saharan

African countries is around 18 to 20 compared to 27 for India and 30 for Brazil. Currently, five of the top 10 fastest growing economies in the world are in Africa, albeit from a low base. Hence the perception of Africa, which in the past has been called the hopeless continent, has completely changed. Now it is regarded as a continent in which you must have a market presence to get away from the flatness of Europe. I participated in a session recently with one of the world's largest cosmetics companies where one of the managers said that Africa is now their Number One target market for new hair and skin-care products as you can only sell so much anti-wrinkle cream in Europe!

As far as options for businesses arising from the grey flag are concerned, plenty of opportunities are available to make money from building and managing retirement villages to selling all those accessories and health-care products that make the lives of old people easier. I have already dealt with the risks associated with the flag.

The anti-establishment flag

We are now back to a cloudy flag with many different end games as was demonstrated in the surprising result of the Greek referendum which overwhelmingly said no to Europe's bailout terms. Of course, the terms were made even more stringent in the subsequent negotiations, which ended in a bailout of €86 billion. Before that, though, no more austerity was the sub-theme of the referendum result. We are now in a world where the middle class is furious with the super-rich. The poor have always been angry but now it is the turn of the middle class.

Looking back in history, it is the members of the middle class that create revolutions. Karl Marx was the son of an attorney and privately educated. Friedrich Engels was the son of a wealthy German cotton textile manufacturer. He met

Marx in 1842 in Berlin and the pair of them produced one of the most famous radical texts of all time in 1848: *The Communist Manifesto*. Previously Maximilien Robespierre was one of the primary leaders of the French Revolution which began in 1792. His father was also a lawyer and Maximilien the son completed his law studies with distinction.

Back in 2002, I co-authored a book with Wayne Visser. At the time, he was Director of Sustainability Services in KPMG South Africa. The book's title was *Beyond Reasonable Greed*. Remember the phrase immortalised by Michael Douglas who played Gordon Gekko in the 1987 movie *Wall Street*? Our thesis was that the world had more than lived up to those words by pursuing the principle that excessive greed is even better. We pointed out that one of the worrying effects of speculative trading was an increase in the volatility and instability of financial markets. Then followed these words: "In turn, by making real economies more unpredictable, these roller-coaster fluctuations destroy the livelihoods of small traders and farmers, increase business bankruptcies and disrupt the plans of supposedly sovereign governments to provide a better life for all."

As a result, we argued strongly that the world should 'shape-shift' from the tooth-and-claw logic of lions to the more caring, holistic philosophy of the elephant.

The underbelly of La Belle Époque

In an economic treatise of 696 pages entitled *Capital in the Twenty-First Century* and published in 2013, a Frenchman called Thomas Piketty applied a more scientific approach to reach the same conclusion as us.

He definitely struck a chord as his book went to the top of the Amazon bestseller chart. He studied tax returns of citizens in Europe and America submitted since the 1880s together with other data in order to arrive at his basic thesis: The prime driving force behind material inequality in society is when the return on capital employed (r) in a country consistently exceeds its economic growth rate (g) over a long period of time. Return on capital is, among other things, derived from corporate profits, interest, dividends, capital appreciation of shares and gains in the value of property.

His prime example is what happened in the 20th Century. At the beginning of it, Europe was experiencing La Belle Époque, or a golden age, where new technologies, scientific discoveries and masterpieces in art, music and literature were commonplace. The period was marked by optimism and peace and ended abruptly in 1914 with the onset of the First World War. However, largely ignored is the fact that there existed a large economic underclass who did not share in the prosperity and good times.

In 1910, the top 1% of the European population earned 20% of the national income; the next 9% earned 30%; the next 40% earned 30% and the bottom 50% earned 20%. In other words, the wealthiest 1% earned as much as the poorest 50%. The cause was unequal ownership of assets, not unequal pay. In those days, it was better to marry into money than get a decent job.

Subsequently, the two world wars as well as the Great Depression destroyed much of the capital of the moneyed aristocracy. Then, from 1945 onwards, 30 years of spectacular economic growth outstripped the return on capital. It also meant a surge in salaries and wages that led to a dramatic fall in the inequality of income by the mid-1970s. By contrast, in the remainder of the last century and the first decade and a half of this one, global economic growth has been more subdued. Hence, the return on capital during this period has considerably exceeded the economic growth rate in most developed economies, and particularly in America.

Patrimonial capitalism

The net result is that the US in 2010 had an income distribution among its population which is equivalent to the figures quoted above for Europe in 1910. Pictorially, there has been a gigantic 'U' in inequality over the last 100 years and we are back to what Piketty calls 'patrimonial capitalism' dominated by oligarchs and inherited wealth. He also adds that the super salaries and bonuses earned by numerous company executives have contributed to the current state of affairs. It is no longer just sports heroes, movie stars and pop musicians making a fortune. It is your run-of-the-mill CEO. At S&P 500 companies in the US, the corporate equivalent to the Gini coefficient, which measures the ratio of the remuneration package of the CEO to the average pay of workers, has risen from a mean of 35 in the 1970s to 373 in 2014. It is now more than 1 000 in some companies. The average worker earned $36 134 in 2014, while compensation for CEOs averaged about $13.5 million. In the UK, the ratio is somewhat lower at 183 but still noteworthy. Also in this avaricious context, Oxfam came up with a startling statistic in 2014: The richest 85 people across the globe have as much wealth as the poorest half of the world's population. You could fit the 85 plutocrats into a small restaurant.

It is interesting to note that for the first time in the modern economic era, the US middle class no longer has the highest income per head in the world. That position is now held by Canada. Obviously, in the billionaire class, America remains in premier place in terms of numbers.

Piketty's recommendation to correct the problem is a global wealth tax of 2% and a progressive income tax structure which rises to 80% at the highest income levels. This is obviously controversial. Many critics argue that such measures would dampen economic growth even further in a world where, as I remarked in the preceding section, ageing demographics are already adversely affecting economic prospects in the fore-seeable future. There is also the fear that the rich will hide their money, while governments will spend the additional revenue inefficiently.

The next middle class revolution

Despite the *Financial Times* querying some of his mathematics, the majority of expert opinion is that Piketty has hit the bullseye with his analysis. A widespread suspicion is out there that all the money created by quantitative easing in America, Europe and Japan has bypassed the real economy and gone straight into equity markets and property. The super-rich with their savings invested in these areas have therefore fully recovered financially from the market crash of 2008. Meanwhile, middle class people, who mainly depend on their salaries or the profit made out of a small business to finance the expense of their daily lives, are still going through hard times. In real terms, salaries have been flat since 2008 as salary increases have merely kept pace with inflation. The recovery has been mild, to say the least.

My prize example is the price of houses in London. The absurd prices paid by foreigners for houses in Kensington, Knightsbridge and Belgravia have ricocheted outwards into the outer suburbs and surrounding counties, making it almost impossible for young British middle-class families to buy their first house in or around their own capital city. So they have to commute from further afield which costs time and money. I was able to buy my first flat in Putney at the age of 25 without too much trouble or assistance from my parents. The current young generation has to be loaded with cash to do that. It may not be an over-exaggeration to say that theirs is the first generation which has less opportunity than their parents of living a reasonable life. We, the oldies, had the best of times.

So anger among the middle class has mounted. In the UK,

Westminster and its politicians are put in the same bracket as big business and super-rich executives. They are part of the Establishment that has to be rocked. Their centrist, moderate policies have led to extremely uneven, immoderate consequences. Brussels and the European Parliament, backed up by an array of well-heeled bureaucrats, inspire similar negative thoughts. It is leading to interesting election results with political parties, which until a few years ago were on the fringe, now on the centre stage. Syriza, with left-wing and communist roots, now governs Greece. The Scottish National Party is now the second biggest opposition party in the House of Commons. They do not want Britain to renew its nuclear deterrent but rather spend the money on housing for the poor. Elections in other countries may follow the same trend as old-fasioned socialism makes a comeback.

People have simply had enough of spin doctors manipulating what politicians say in order to please as many constituencies as possible and to avoid being politically incorrect. They are fed up with expense scandals and other examples of the real life imperfections of politicians that cut right across the ideals that they urge the electorate to live their own life by. They hate political speak where politicians look terribly serious on TV as they say nothing at all because everything is qualified to the point of being meaningless. They see through the empty promises made of extra expenditure on welfare programmes while cutting taxes. They reluctantly acknowledge that the contradiction between the two policies will result in the rise and rise of public debt, another flag to come. They shrug their shoulders when compromises are made by the politicians to turn the impossible into the possible. They knew it all along.

Washington, Whitehall and Canberra are at their lowest level in popular ranking in years. I am not for one moment saying all politicians are corrupt, inept or morally bankrupt but their brand has taken a huge hit. It makes life for the ones that are honest, hard-working and genuinely concerned about creating a better quality of life for the broad swathe of their citizens a lot more difficult. Thus, we have the rise of new figures in the political domain who epitomise the expression: "I am what I am. Take me or leave me." This is greeted with total mystification and amazement by the media and political gurus who are accustomed to the double meanings and ambivalence of the existing generation of politicians.

We are entering a new world of politics where the platform of social media is creating unexpected heroes and heroines out of ordinary individuals who have for a long time been consigned to the back benches. The anti-establishment flag is promoting them to the front bench and a position of great influence over human affairs. Jeremy Corbyn, leader of the Labour Party in the UK, and Bernie Sanders, who is a presidential candidate for the Democratic Party in the US, are two examples of this megatrend. They are both grumpy old men but totally honest and candid in how they would set things right. Corbyn had the lowest expenses claim of any MP in the House of Commons in 2010 and I particularly like Sanders' point that education is better than incarceration! Their lack of celebrity up till now is their real weapon to unseat the establishment. Their public meetings remind one of the atmosphere of Led Zeppelin concerts in the 1970s. Meanwhile, Donald Trump, the leading Republican presidential candidate in the US at the moment, is at the opposite end of the political spectrum to Corbyn and Sanders. Despite being a brash billionaire who makes the most outrageous and insensitive comments on a variety of issues, he has gained popularity precisely because he is not seen as part of the Washington political or donor establishment. He may not last long in the presidential race, but he has irrevocably changed its dynamic.

There has also been quite a change of attitude about the ethics of financial management. Tax avoidance is now put into the same category as tax evasion, as many American companies, which do business in the UK but steer their profits into lower tax countries, have found out to their detriment. Their actions have attracted very negative publicity and even a call to boycott their goods. Celebrities who avoid tax by participating in schemes that are on the edge of the law are now being named and shamed, much to their embarrassment and cost to their reputation. Tax havens everywhere are under the spotlight and the kind of secrecy in banking that has protected the super-rich for so many years is fast being eroded.

For business surveying its options in light of this flag, it could be a rocky road. The anti-austerity movement – for that read the anti-establishment movement – is on the march. They want Piketty's 'g' to be higher than the 'r' and quality of life to be accompanied by equality of life as it did in the middle of the last century. We of course must debate in South Africa the issue of income inequality which rates alongside poverty and unemployment as our biggest scourge. You will see in the last section that I believe in an inclusive economy with equal opportunity for all aspiring entrepreneurs in order to achieve Piketty's goal of greater equality of outcome. A modern version of Beatrice Webb, who was a staunch Fabian, would be shaking Piketty's hand for the contribution he has made to the dismal science of economics.

The green flag

This is the quintessential slow-rising flag that has been ignored for so long because we as the human race are not genetically tuned to responding to trends that creep up on us. Or we are in a state of self-denial. It is the flag of climate change as well as the flag of general destruction which we are wreaking on our environment because of our success in reproducing ourselves. A great metaphor for the planet is a spacecraft, nonetheless a very large one. The reason is that a spacecraft has a finite amount of room, limited food, water and other necessities for the astronauts to survive on and limited waste-disposal facilities. Everybody understands that a spaceship is a closed system.

Not so the Earth. Somehow your average inhabitant on it treats it as a boundless resource that will last till eternity. I was given a statistic the other day that if the Chinese were ever to reach America's standard of living, you would need four Spaceship Earths. But we only have one Spaceship Earth. Imagine what you would do as an astronaut if another member of the crew was endangering the whole spacecraft in the way in which he behaved. You would have words with him and, if he did not listen, you would kick him out. Cumulatively, Americans have had more effect on living conditions inside the spacecraft than any other nation.

I was introduced to the green flag when I co-authored a book on the environment in 1989. Entitled *South African Environments into the 21st Century*, my co-authors were the highly respected ecologists Brian Huntley and Roy Siegfried. In the concluding chapter of the book, we made the following statement: "The answer is that life is multidimensional. At the core of sustainable development lies economic growth, the state of the environment and the quality of human life. Each of these three dimensions is essential for the other two to exist. But each does not guarantee the existence of the others. Quite the reverse – going too far in one direction endangers the others. So the three dimensions have to be kept constantly and concurrently in mind."

My next involvement with this flag took place in London in 2006. I was asked to help some of the world's top climate experts build a set of scenarios ahead of the summit in Bali in December 2007. They came up with the scenario matrix shown overleaf:

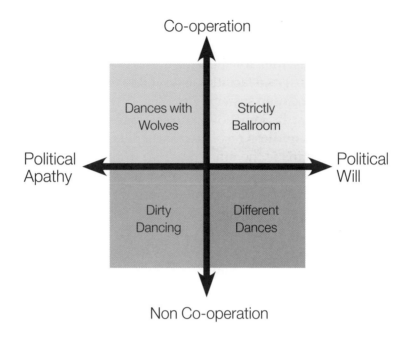

Co-operation

Dances with
Wolves

Strictly
Ballroom

Political
Apathy

Political
Will

Dirty
Dancing

Different
Dances

Non Co-operation

The lower half of the matrix represented the pre-Bali situation where nations were doing their own thing because no agreement was in place. 'Dirty Dancing' was the quadrant occupied by nations which had made no effort at all to stem their carbon dioxide emissions. 'Different Dances' was the quadrant filled by players making some effort to use alternative energy sources in a move away from the consumption of fossil fuels including coal. Nuclear, hydro, wind, solar and geothermal were put in the alternative energy category. Unfortunately, most advanced and developing nations were assigned to Dirty Dancing and only a handful of European countries and California as a state were considered to be making progress in learning to dance differently.

The upper half of the matrix consisted of two possible scenarios after the Bali summit. 'Dances with Wolves' was an agreement reached with much fanfare but little substance. It offered no specific incentives on the one hand or penalties on the other hand to compel the dirty dancers or wolves to change their behaviour. It was business as usual with no reduction at all in carbon dioxide emissions and probably an overall increase due to the expanding power requirements of the developing world including China and India.

'Strictly Ballroom' was the virtuous outcome where a tight agreement with measurable outcomes was formulated and accepted by the Bali summit. Thereafter everyone waltzed in time to it, particularly the super-emitters like America and China. When I asked them to give a probability to the two scenarios, they put 95% odds on Dances with Wolves and 5% on Strictly Ballroom. One delegate said that it would require seven hurricanes, all as powerful as Hurricane Katrina, to hit seven different American cities in a row for Capitol Hill to realise that Mother Nature could be more devastating than a human enemy – and take the issue seriously.

In answer to another question I put to them about the probability of man-made emissions being responsible for climate change as opposed to it being part of a natural cycle, they said that in a criminal court of law they would give mankind a guilty verdict because it was beyond reasonable doubt. The carbon dioxide concentration in our atmosphere was now at a record level and if you went back 160 000 years by analysing Antarctic ice cores, there was a clear correlation between carbon dioxide concentration and the change in the mean global surface temperature. In 1890, a Swede called Svante Arrhenius had drawn attention to the possible long-term impact that the coal-dependent Industrial Revolution would have on the global climate. His surmise was almost certainly right; and to this should be added the reduction in photosynthetic uptake of carbon dioxide caused by the cutting down of the world's forests, which are the Earth's lungs.

Deforestation has already destroyed 90% of West Africa's rainforests and two-thirds of Madagascar's forests. It could wipe out 60% of the Amazon forest by 2030, while Indonesia may be logged out in 10 years. The loss of these forests is estimated to contribute between 12 and 15% to annual greenhouse emissions, equivalent to the combined emissions of all trains, planes and cars in the world.

Despite all this, the actual result of the Bali conference in 2007 confirmed the worst expectations of the participants in my London session.

A change of tune

My last major encounter regarding the green flag was in 2012 at a function in Johannesburg where the host was an American Ivy League university and the attendees were South Africans who had done courses there. Various members of the faculty gave lectures and I was the external guest speaker. I gave my presentation on scenarios and flags after which a young American woman who had just joined the faculty came up to me. She said that her previous post was in the scenario planning team at an agency looking after homeland security. They had painted scenarios but never used flags. When I enquired how they convinced the American President of the authenticity of a scenario without mentioning flags, she said with a grin: "When he asked what the probability of a scenario was, we collectively said 100%!" She believed the addition of flags would provide a much better technique to calibrate the probability of a scenario, and I hear the agency has added flagwatching to its bag of analytical tools.

I then remarked that I did not often talk to someone who advised the American President on national threats and, without her spilling secrets, what were they? The prime threat was unsurprisingly terrorism; but she did make the prophetic comment that the threat had changed from an external strike like 9/11 (which she felt the US had taken adequate precautions against) to the scenario of internal harm through self-radicalisation of America's own citizens. This was before the bombings at the end of the Boston Marathon in 2013.

But it was the second threat that nearly made me fall off my chair: climate change. I expressed amazement as many Americans regarded climate change as a myth and dismissed the inconvenient truths put forward by Al Gore. Yet, here she was saying it was the second biggest security threat to America. She replied in the affirmative and added that, to use my terminology, there were three sub-flags to indicate that the threat should be taken seriously.

The first sub-flag was temperature. Various institutions in the US had databases going back more than 50 years. The vast bulk of the data suggested a 1°C increase in surface temperatures over the last 50 years. Yes, there were places where temperatures were flat or had even declined; and these were used by the dissidents to debase the whole theory of global warming. But, on balance of evidence, temperatures had risen. Then she made another prophetic comment: the first country to feel the real heat of climate change would be Australia. Subsequently, 2013 and 2014 have been the hottest years in Australia's history and there is now a serious worry around rising evaporation rates affecting the volume of water flowing in rivers through central Australia. Water may become Australia's most precious resource if it is not already so. I was at the mouth of the Murray River south of Adelaide the other day and it is tiny for the country's longest river. It has to be constantly dredged to maintain a minimal flow from and to the sea. Equally, given the drier conditions, bush fires may increase in number and in the area they destroy.

Australian meteorologists have just added the colour deep purple to their weather maps for places where the temperature is above 50°C. I remember taking a light aircraft into the

Kimberley Plateau in the North West of Australia where the temperature occasionally approaches 50°C. We had lunch in a farmstead with an especially thick ceiling to withstand the heat. Approaching the farmstead, I felt I was walking in a microwave and was conscious of the fact that I was a 37-degree animal in a 45-degree environment.

Incidentally, it is thought that the only beneficiaries of the temperature flag could be Russia and Canada as the frozen territory in their higher latitudes is gradually converted into arable land and new shipping lanes are opened up around their northern coasts. The downside is that the thawing of the permafrost in these regions could release large quantities of methane, a greenhouse gas, into the atmosphere and worsen the situation.

The second sub-flag, she said, was rising sea levels due to the melting of the Arctic and Antarctic, particularly the latter. If whole ice shelves began falling off the edge of the Antarctic, the sea level could rise half a metre. In America, two cities were at real risk: New Orleans, half of which is below sea level, and Miami, which has a tidal surge along the coast like the Bristol Channel. However, she said the countries at most risk were the small island groups in the Indian Ocean. I go regularly to Mauritius and I have for some time been encouraging the authorities there to measure the sea levels around the coast. Tourism is a major part of their economy and most of the hotels are sited on the coastline.

California dreaming now a nightmare

The third sub-flag was the one she felt would change the American public's attitude towards climate change. It was the increasing frequency and amplitude of extreme weather events. She carefully chose the word 'amplitude' to indicate that the pendulum would be swinging more widely between extremely cold and extremely hot events, as a result of the greater amount of energy in the atmosphere. Brian, Roy and I anticipated her third sub-flag in our 1989 book with the following words: "The rise in frequency and scale of extreme events like droughts, floods, hailstorms and hurricanes – which would occur as the global climate moved through a series of temporary states to a new equilibrium – would have a severe impact on infrastructure, agriculture and reinsurance."

The year 2015 will go down as a horrible year for America in regard to the third sub-flag. It started with a record blizzard at the end of January in Boston, Massachusetts, followed by record floods in May in Texas. But, from the chats I had with passengers on the cruise earlier this year, the event that comes across as a real game-changer to me was the drought in California. In its fourth year at the time of writing this, some experts believe it could be around for as long as 40 years, outlasting the Dustbowl Drought of the 1930s on the Great Plains. Three million people left their farms during that historic drought.

Already, life in California has become pretty extreme. For the first time in 75 years, there was no snow up north to replenish the reservoirs. There are towns in the middle of the state which have literally run out of water and it has to be brought in on a daily basis. Fish have to be trucked up the rivers because there is not enough water for them to swim upstream to spawn. The latest projection is that if the drought drags on for another four years, the wild populations of some of California's most prized fish will vanish, including the salmon. Governor Jerry Brown has ordered a 25% reduction in state-wide water use, which has drawn an angry response from the farmers with water rights that go back to the founding of the state. They feel that water is something that God supplies and nobody should get between them and God. Meanwhile, fires can be set off with a single spark and many fireworks displays to celebrate the 4th of July in 2015 were cancelled. Nevertheless, the number of Californian wild fires so far in 2015 is well above the annual norm. In Los Angeles, drones are being flown over the suburbs to see whether celebrities are complying with the restrictions. Barbra Streisand and the Kardashians have been the first targets of drought-shaming after having their lush green gardens exposed by the press. Tom Selleck has settled a dispute with a nearby water district after they reportedly discovered his ranch, which lies outside their borders, was getting regular deliveries by truck from one of their own public hydrants.

Probably the most surprising feature of the drought is that Silicon Valley, which has an overload of the brightest minds in the world, has added little if no value in coming up with innovative approaches to water management. Instead, the state government has sought advice from Israelis and Australians on possible solutions to their water problems.

The key sub-flag to watch now is the outcome of the next climate change summit in Paris in December 2015. Barack Obama is on the warpath. He has put the negotiation of a genuine agreement limiting carbon dioxide emissions on his list of to-do items before he steps down as President. To lead by example, he has already issued a new rule requiring a 32% cut in such emissions from US power plants by 2030 from levels existing in 2005. The intention is for the nation to get 28% of its electricity from renewable resources by 2030 as opposed to roughly 13% in 2014. He has also signed a deal with China as they and America are the two largest national emitters in the world. Pope Francis has added his voice to the new dialogue by calling Earth 'an immense pile of filth'. That is strong language indeed to use in an Encyclical. As sinners who created the pile of filth, we can only go up from where the Pope has placed us. Maybe, Strictly Ballroom will become a reality this time around. My surmise is that at some time in the future every product will have to have its total carbon footprint from womb to tomb on its label, including its packaging and freight. We may even have to declare our personal carbon footprint on an annual basis. That could perturb all those environmentalists, or 'lamborgreenies' as they are known, who jet around the world attending climate change conferences.

The Stamford Plaza hotel in Adelaide, Australia, has done its bit to reduce the carbon footprint of its guests in a clever way. You get 10 Australian dollars off your food and beverage bill if you choose not to have your room serviced when you are spending more than one night at the hotel. Even the washing of sheets and towels has a carbon footprint that can be avoided with a financial incentive.

Before moving on from the green flag, I must mention a book called *The Sixth Extinction: An Unnatural History* by Elizabeth Colbert. The book is about mass extinctions of species in the history of our planet and the one we are currently experiencing. Asteroids may have killed the dinosaurs in the Fifth Extinction but human activity is to blame for the present one. After drawing attention to the fact that amphibians are the world's most endangered class of animals, she writes: "But also heading towards extinction are one-third of all reef-building corals, a third of all fresh-water molluscs, a third of sharks and rays, a quarter of all mammals, a fifth of all reptiles and sixth of all birds."

I would like to add bees to her list because they are disappearing in America, Europe and China. It is connected to colony collapse disorder, a mysterious disease upsetting honeybee hives. A combination of pesticides and disease are thought to be the reason.

In short, there is more to the green flag than climate change. And we cannot just barge other species out of our spaceship to make more room for ourselves. Who knows what our life will be like if we destroy the intricate patterns of nature? Somewhere down the line our spaceship may become uninhabitable. Ultimately, therefore, measures to restrict population growth may become more acceptable, as the Moon and Mars are not attractive alternatives.

As I said earlier on, it now takes us 12 years to do what it took 200 000 years from the beginning of mankind till 1810 to do: Create one billion extra voyagers on the spaceship. Even with urbanisation, improving living standards and the rising cost of having a child slowing population growth, the latest UN projection for 2100 is a world population of 11.2 billion compared to 7.3 billion in 2015. Africa and Asia together will make up 83% of that figure, based on current trends of fertility. By contrast, the West, made up of Europe and North America, will descend to a minority of 10%. Whatever the make-up of the human race, being the dominant species on a spaceship spinning out of control with too many passengers means absolutely nothing.

The national debt flag

This flag is linked to the grey flag, but unlike the latter it carries a wide range of possible consequences and is therefore cloudy. Let us begin with Japan which has the highest ratio of national debt to GDP in the world. It stands at 230% when the recommended maximum according to the European Union is 60%. Has there been an uproar over the profligacy of the Japanese government? The answer is no. The reason is that less than 5% of Japanese public debt is held by foreign countries. The Japanese themselves are great savers and are willing to lend their savings to their own government.

Greece's national debt sits at 177% of GDP which is a much lower percentage than Japan. The difficulty is that most of the Greek debt is owed to lenders beyond its borders. Greece's ratio compares to the one for Italy at 132%, Spain at 98%, France at 95%, the UK at 89% and Germany at 75%. Notice all these ratios are above the recommended ceiling of 60%. The US sits at 101% because the US government owes its lenders locally and overseas more than $18 trillion. The last time the US was over 100% was during the Second World War. Thanks to consistently high economic growth after the war, the ratio dived to a reasonable level for the remainder of the last century; but in the last 10 years it has soared again. The Scandinavian countries are all below 50%, Australia is 29% and Russia is 18%. South Africa's debt to GDP ratio is 44%.

The whole point of quoting these figures is to justify the statement that the grey flag is causing governments in many countries to borrow more than they should. With interest rates at virtually zero (lower than they have ever been in the last 300 years), the situation can be handled in most cases. The problem will only come when interest rates turn up, if they ever do. Then, money will have to be diverted from other parts of the national budget to service the increased cost of borrowing. For example, a 2% jump in the interest rate on the current US national debt of $18 trillion would raise annual interest payments by the federal government by an additional $360 billion. By any standards, that is an astronomical amount of money.

The analogy I use to indicate the risk of an easy money policy is that you don't know whether a patient in ICU will stage a full recovery until you have removed the drips. In the case of the world economy, the drip is zero interest rates. Let's see what happens if and when the drip is halted. Perhaps you will find it was the wrong medication from the start.

A Greek odyssey

Greece in itself is a red flag because their real economy is in a parlous state and they cannot repay their national debt even as things stand. The Greek population is just over 11 million and has begun to decline in numbers. The over 65s are 19% of that figure and this is estimated to rise to 23% in 2025. At present, workers can retire at the relatively low age of 57, if they so wish, and receive a full pension. Almost 18% of Greece's GDP goes on pensions, the highest proportion in Europe. It is expected the retirement age will shortly be raised to a figure in the mid to late 60s. Germany, by comparison, has a retirement age of 67 and naturally many of their citizens are fuming about the fact that their country is lending Greece money to pay its pensioners when Germans are still working in their 60s.

In my last book *21st Century Megatrends*, I made the following comment in an introduction to a *News24* article entitled "Eurowinked": "I also wanted to highlight the danger of moral hazard, where you get seduced into taking a risk because you think that part of the risk is laid off on other parties. If Greece had been a stand-alone nation, many of the banks would have seen the true risks of lending money to it. However, as a member of an exclusive European club, Greece had access to the goodwill of the other members who were blind to its real weaknesses."

That is why we have such a mess today. Moreover, lending Greece another €86 billion with the strict conditions imposed by the latest bailout package could compound the problem and lead to a Eurogeddon scenario. The IMF estimates that, without large-scale debt relief, Greece's debt-to-GDP ratio will rise to 200% by 2017. And life for Greeks could become intolerable. They are on an odyssey worthy of the one written by Homer. One hopes their fortunes will change for the better. But, like Sparta of old, they may have to accept some austerity.

I believe the old Common Market was a viable concept for Europe, but the addition of a common currency was a step too far. The gold standard failed because most currencies had a fixed rate against the US dollar which in turn was supported by gold at a fixed price ($35 an ounce for a long time). Nations could not devalue their currencies to boost their economies, so in the end the system was abolished by mutual agreement. The euro could go the same way as there is such a difference between the competitiveness of the Eurozone members, but no flexibility to handle it.

In business terms, the European Union reminds me of a gigantic conglomerate without a group CEO. Each country has its own CEO but, unlike America where the governors of the individual states acknowledge the US President as the overall leader, Europe has nothing similar in its structure. Brussels simply lacks the kind of authority invested in the US Presidency and therefore all major decisions on Europe's future have to be negotiated and agreed on by the national heads of state in a summit meeting.

The Eurozone has 19 members and the European Union 28. That is a serious number of delegates from which to obtain consensus. Where an individual head of state is at variance with the consensus of the national leaders, there is no equivalent to a group CEO to haul him (or her) into line and say: "This is the way it is." His retort will be that he is representing his own citizens (or shareholders in the corporate metaphor) because he was elected by them and nobody can surpass that. So, Europe would have to become the United States of Europe with full political union as well as fiscal and economic union to have a consistent strategy in protecting its own interests. Given the different cultures, languages and histories of the European Union members, that is an unlikely scenario at the present time.

Notwithstanding my pessimism, I would like to quote a line from *The Iliad*, Homer's first poem: "There is strength in the union of even sorry men."

The misnomer of contagion

One of the words used again and again is 'contagion'. Apart from it being an emotionally loaded word, it is used to support the following argument. If Greece defaults on its loans and gets away with it, that concession will send a message to other borrowers like Portugal, Spain and Italy that they can do the same. Moreover, Spain and Italy have a much bigger loan book to default on. However, the logic is flawed in that the word 'contagion' implies that a person infected by a disease can infect other people who at the moment are perfectly healthy.

The statistics provided in the second paragraph on this flag clearly indicate that most of the big economic players are suffering from the same affliction as Greece in regard to over-borrowing by the state, but not in such an extreme form. The explanation for this is that they are all democracies and the last thing you do as an elected government is implement policies which could motivate your supporters to cast their votes in the next election for another party. Hence, you avoid austerity programmes like the plague. Everybody knows that cutting welfare expenditure and raising taxes is potentially a formula for committing suicide at the ballot box. Thus, it is much easier politically to run a budget deficit and finance it through further borrowings.

The grey flag is pitted against the anti-establishment flag. On the one hand, the ageing of national populations in the advanced economies of Europe and Japan is slowing global GDP growth. This is diminishing the probability of the kind of economic miracle that came after the Second World War, where high economic growth expanded the divisor in the national-debt to-GDP ratio and painlessly reduced the ratio. On the other hand, the pressure on governments to increase public spending on health is growing on account of the greater numbers of elderly people. Furthermore, politicians are fully aware of the drive towards a more caring and fair society inherent in lowering the anti-establishment flag. When you have the two conflicting trends illustrated in this case, it can play out in different ways in different countries.

If too many countries cave in and pursue irresponsible policies which escalate their national-debt-to- GDP ratios to record levels, there could be a day of reckoning like the crash of 2008. According to ancient Greek literature, hubris (arrogance) is inevitably followed by nemesis (retribution). In this case, the arrogance of governments believing that they are not subject to the normal laws of borrowing could eventually lead to their downfall. But I'll say more about that later when I describe the 'Forked Lightning' scenario.

The world of work flag

This is a clockwork flag that has been ticking away since the 1960s. In my book *The World and South Africa in the 1990s*, I made the following comment: "Through microelectronics, the world is designing labour out of the big manufacturing systems and forcing a movement towards service occupations. In the 1950s, 30% of the assembly cost of a car was labour. That figure has fallen to between 7 and 8% as a result of robotics and automated production lines."

For good measure, I added: "In the late 1920s, half of Americans were employed as farmers and blue-collar manufacturers. The figures today are startling. Around 3% of Americans are farmers and 15% are blue-collar manufacturers. About 95% of the new jobs created in the United States in the last 10 years have been in the service sector of the economy. The latter now employs 73% of the US workforce." The last figure is close to 80% today.

The trend is as clear and precise as Big Ben, the famous clock at Westminster in London. But, unlike Big Ben, the booming chimes of the trend have not been heard in the hallowed halls of the best universities and schools in the world, let alone by any well-known expert in the field of education. Curricula are truly academic these days because they are of no earthly use to pupils and students for finding work in the job market of today. When I was at school and university in England in the 1960s, bright young people got A-levels at school and a passable degree at university and then waved their certificates in front of the recruitment departments of the civil service and big companies. That got them a job alongside thousands of other people with a common ambition to climb the corporate ladder.

Those days are gone forever for the vast majority of young work-seekers today except for the lucky ones who can still find a career in the companies that are not retrenching staff, in state departments that are not running out of money and professions like accounting, law, medicine and teaching. Even then the jobs may not carry the same level of security in terms of defined pension benefits, medical aid and the guarantee of life-time employment.

Technological advances in machinery have driven a stake through many jobs as I have already indicated, to which one might add the internet, tablets and mobile phones. Moreover, companies have cut down on the number of permanent employees as they restrict their recruitment to posts dedicated to the core activities of the business. The rest of the non-core activities are subcontracted to people on fixed-term contracts or smaller enterprises specialising in those functions. This gives the big company flexibility in increasing or decreasing their overall workforce in line with market conditions.

For example, when I was CEO of Anglo's Gold and Uranium Division in the early 1990s, the gold mines falling under the division's umbrella employed around 220 000 staff. We did everything on the mines ourselves including security, food preparation for the miners and management of the hospitals associated with the mines. We had enough leeway to subsidise the poor shafts with the extra profit from the rich shafts to keep everybody employed. Today, the total employment of the entire gold mining industry is 119 000 and there is less latitude for stopping retrenchments. Obviously, part of the decline is due to shafts shutting down because the gold-bearing orebody has been exhausted. But it is symptomatic of so many other industries in manufacturing and the service sector as they seek to improve productivity. Their employment figures are dwindling which is bad news for the trade union movement whose sole purpose is to protect workers in the formal sector. The world of mass employment, which makes them a relevant and important player, is fast disappearing.

The global youth unemployment rate is estimated to be around 13%, ranging from 22% in the European Union to 11% in East Asia. In South Africa, Greece and Spain, the rate is around 50% which is reckoned to be the highest in the world in countries where official statistics are kept. Italy stands at 42%. A 2013 cover of *The Economist* featured the words 'Generation jobless' and the accompanying article indicated that the word 'job' is rapidly becoming like the word 'dinosaur' for aspirant job seekers. The overall rate of unemployment in South Africa stands at close to 25% which was the peak unemployment rate in America during the Great Depression. Right now in America, the overall unemployment rate is 5.1% down from 10% in October 2009. They are creating around 250 000 jobs a month but the nature of these jobs has changed.

The term used in America these days is 'informal employment'. It is not synonymous with working in the informal sector, which lies outside the purview of the government and is largely untaxed. Instead, informal employment applies mainly to contract labour working for big and small businesses. Indeed, the latest estimate is that the small business sector in the US is responsible for creating 80% of the new jobs there. In the UK, there are over one million 'zero hour' workers who wait for the phone to ring at home with the request by a company that they fill in for someone who hasn't reported for work because of ill health or for other reasons.

The age of entrepreneurship

The bottom line is that young people have to create jobs for themselves rather than find jobs. Hence, the spotlight has moved from expanding formal employment opportunities in the public and private sector to enterprise creation by entrepreneurs. When politicians and trade unionists talk about decent work or decent jobs, they are completely ignoring this trend or flag. In this new world of work, your pay and other conditions of employment are what you make them through your own performance and effort.

The latest fad is pop-up retail. You pop up one day as a shop at a temporary venue, then disappear after a few weeks. The Swedish daughter-in-law of one of my friends in London opened a pop-up restaurant in Covent Garden for six weeks over the Christmas period for Swedish tourists visiting the capital city. She hired a chef and out-of-work members of the acting profession as waiters. She had Swedish décor in the restaurant and constructed a menu which would appeal to the taste of her clientele. She set up a website for bookings and away she went. I met her halfway through the life of her pop-up enterprise. She said the thing that surprised her most was that her profit was mainly derived from the drinks she sold to accompany the meal.

Another wonderful example of creating a job was a young man in Windhoek who made toilet paper. When I asked him how he could compete against the global brands, his response was that he made customised toilet paper. When I enquired what that meant, he said that he had learnt how to print photographs on toilet rolls and he had two questions for his customers: "Who is your worst enemy and do you have a photograph?"

In Australia, Uber – the Californian company which invented the app that allows consumers with smartphones to request rides from drivers who own their own cars – is on track to becoming one of the country's top 20 employers, except that Uber employees are usually their own bosses deciding on their own hours of work. Airbnb does for home-owners what Uber does for car owners. It allows them to make money out of their homes by renting them out via the website. As a host, you can charge your guests different prices for different seasons and different-length stays. Both websites have liberated millions of people to start their own businesses by using two of their own assets: a car and a house.

Can you name me any educational institution – be it a school, university or business school – which has taken this flag into consideration and has made the teaching of entre-preneurship its top priority? Can you name me a school where pupils run real businesses which are monitored and where they are given practical advice on how to select a potentially profitable product or service, how to turn themselves into a marketable brand and how to keep a proper set of accounts? I know of only two schools which have done this: The Wyke-ham Collegiate in Pietermaritzburg and Hilton College close by, the inspiration in both cases being a teacher named Ann Kriel. For the rest, they concentrate solely on their students obtaining good grades in their final exam.

The one country that has embraced this flag is Germany. In their teens, pupils can choose between completing their school career in the conventional academic sense or attend-ing schools where the emphasis is on vocational and tech-nical training. Crucially, there is not the kind of snootiness in Germany for the second type of education that exists in a Britain. The result is that the youth unemployment rate in Germany is 7.1%, nearly half the global rate and lower than the rate in virtually any other advanced economy. It is such a shame that the technical school route was almost aban-doned in South Africa after 1994. I earnestly hope that it is revived because school leavers with technical skills have a higher chance of starting their own businesses and sustaining them.

Governments have only one option in coping with this flag. They must create an environment that is fully supportive of small business and is free of the kind of bureaucracy that retards its growth. They must ensure that the economy is sufficiently inclusive for small players to co-exist alongside the big players. In fact, they should work towards a dual-logic economy, where small companies become part of the supply chain of big companies and the two develop a harmonious relationship. In the 1980s, Pierre Wack was a visiting professor at Harvard Business School as well as a consultant to Anglo American. During one of his stays in Boston, he asked me to come across to give a lecture at the school on my experience of using scenarios to change the conversation in South Africa. I stayed at the Dean's lodge on campus; and the dean kindly threw a dinner for me to meet members of the faculty. I remember asking them at the dinner whether any of them had run a real business before joining the school. There was a general shaking of heads and my point then was that some real business experience could go a long way. Now, I would go further. Nothing in my Anglo career prepared me for running my own small consultancy where I do everything myself. Hence, I can now confirm that the only way you learn how to become an entrepreneur is to be one.

The porous border flag

This is a cloudy flag because no one can predict the path it will take as it unfurls. As an immigrant myself, the flag holds a certain fascination.

Back in 1992, I published a book called *The New Century* in which I wrote the following: "Immigration is set to become the thorniest issue of the 1990s in America and Europe. In the US, the more open relationship developing with Mexico is likely to increase the flow of immigrants, legal and illegal, into states such as California. Such levels of immigration will eventually alter the composition of US society in a significant way. By 2025 Spanish-speaking people will form the largest minority in America. Indeed, the word 'minority' will by then be inappropriate as American society will have evolved to a position where it will be multiracial and multicultural.

"Hard and soft liberals converge in their attitudes towards immigration. Hard liberals believe that immigrants help keep the labour market flexible; soft liberals value the cultural diversity that immigrants bring. Both underplay the social strains that creep into society as it becomes more disparate, strains which could conceivably erode the sense of national purpose as well as national community. The 'melting pot' theory which held that the Great American Dream would mould people into true Americans looks distinctly ragged around the edges.

"For a start, people are arguing about what constitutes a 'true American'. Should he or she be like you or me? Should children be taught to become European, African, Spanish or Asian Americans? – or a little bit of each? The problem is that most ordinary people grow up with one language, one culture, one history predominating in their lives, with perhaps a smattering of knowledge about the others. The strongest social forces in their lives are their family, school and immediate neighbourhood – not society at large. And when these schools and neighbourhoods are, for the most part, monocultural – a mosaic of separate Italian, African, Korean, Latin, Old-Protestant-European communities – the American glue begins to come unstuck. Each immigrant is pigeon-holed into his or her own clan rather than absorbed into the wider community.

"For all the apprehensions expressed, American society is infinitely adaptable. It may well find in the long run innovative ways of re-inspiring sufficiently broad loyalties to overarch the clannish divisions. After all, the United States is still united. Ultimately the 'American way' rubs off on any new immigrant: The esprit de corps of belonging to the greatest nation on Earth is very catching. Perhaps the fire under the 'melting pot' merely needs rekindling so that the ingredients which have started to separate out come together again. The most effective way of doing this is a reasonable standard of living for everybody.

"On the other side of the Atlantic Ocean, Europe is more brittle, more old-fashioned and quite schizophrenic about immigration. Europeans sympathise, but they don't want to be inundated. As one 'poor young billion' affirmed: The straightest line between my present condition and being part of the developed world is to get there."

Alas, the 2015 riots in Ferguson, Missouri, and Baltimore, Maryland, after the killing of unarmed black men by the police, together with the terrible church massacre in Charleston, South Carolina, which left nine black members of the congregation dead, are a sign that there is a long way to go in fulfilling the American dream. At least, the confederacy flag with all its associations with slavery has been removed from the statehouse grounds of South Carolina.

The Interpol perspective

A little over six years ago in 2009, I was a speaker at a conference convened by Interpol in Paris to examine the changing nature of international crime. It was attended by top police officers from around the world. My assignment was to show how scenario planning could be used to outfox the best criminal minds. Coincidentally, one of the main purposes of the conference was to rank the principal threats to global society posed by the criminals.

Given what I had written 17 years before, I was not surprised by the threat that ranked highest in the mind of the attendees at the time – porous borders or the fact that criminals with deadly intent could enter any country they wanted to in order to pursue their particular brand of criminal activity. The subject of illegal immigrants came up at the same time and one participant corroborated my view that it would become the thorniest of issues by saying: "Of course borders are a temporary phenomenon created several hundred years ago. Before that, you had the great migrations where whole groups of people simply upped sticks and migrated to a different part of the world. Empires came and went. Now you have seven billion residents on this Earth, lots of whom feel cooped up in their present location and want a better quality of life elsewhere."

Two border crossings were identified as being the most porous in the world. The first was the US/Mexican border. As one American delegate said: "We have the most sophisticated technology you can imagine at the official border posts to catch any illegal immigrant trying to get in, but you go 10 miles on either side of those posts and we are totally vulnerable. In the old days, they used to swim across the Rio Grande. Now they tunnel. When you close one down, another one is started several miles away." Illegal immigration is therefore an issue on which Obama walks a tightrope.

The second border was not so much a border as a crossing. The Mediterranean Sea, between Libya and Sicily or Corsica, was considered to be the most accessible route into Europe. Once in Italy itself, it was agreed that the immigrant was free to go anywhere in the European Union, with or without a visa or passport. All this conversation took place before the downfall of Muammar Gaddafi and the descent of Libya into a chaotic state.

Now we have the daily tragedy of hundreds of people setting out from Africa for a better life in Europe in unseaworthy vessels after paying some unscrupulous trafficker a large sum in dollars up front. They either drown or, if they are fortunate, they are rescued by Italian patrol boats. The immigrants do not just originate from Libya, but a whole host of countries in northern Africa. Nearly half of a million immigrants have already made it across the small patch of sea to Europe in 2015, while 2 600 have tragically drowned. The situation looks like it is getting worse as it is rumoured that there are millions of desperate people waiting to take the trip. A Balkan corridor via Greece, Macedonia, Serbia and Hungary has also opened up. The blame game has already started with the accusation that the current problem was engineered by the West's irresponsible meddling to bring about regime change in several African countries including Libya.

Another flashpoint is the port of Calais in France where thousands of migrants are encamped and trying to board trucks and ferries bound for the UK. The truck drivers are genuinely scared as there have been instances of violent protest and physical intimidation. The Eurostar train service has also been disrupted. The plan is to build a huge fence to create a security zone for the trucks and keep the migrants away from the vital transport arteries including the Channel Tunnel. But it is no long-term solution as the movement of goods by road between France and the UK has already been seriously compromised.

Meanwhile, a few European politicians are advocating a tougher approach, like the Australian one, namely the only way to stem the flow is to deny people any chance of actually getting ashore on the mainland. This ignores the fact that Australia is protected by a great deal of ocean. The Mediterranean is a strip by comparison. The other option being considered is military action against the traffickers, but that is likely to involve drone strikes which are becoming increasingly unpopular on account of collateral damage.

The refugee argument

An alternative strategy is being promoted by some prominent non-profit organisations, one or two with close links to the United Nations. All these people are refugees and should be welcomed with open arms by European countries. In fact, the argument goes, Europe is about to make the same mistake as many countries did in the 1930s and early 1940s when they prevented the flight of Jews from Nazi-occupied territory. Having said that, the plight of Syrians fleeing the civil war in their homeland seems to be changing the minds of the public in Germany, their destination of choice. The humanitarian response there is awesome, but will it spread to other countries in the region and for how long if the numbers grow and grow?

The counter argument is that criminals and terrorists will have a field day as they mix in with the mass of immigrants. In addition, health services, which are already stretched, will become totally overwhelmed. The difference between a refugee and an economic migrant has yet to be precisely defined even though there have been countless court cases. In other words, how bad does it have to get in the country of origin to qualify as a refugee?

The flag at the Interpol conference is now flying high and is not going to come down any time soon for many of the affluent nations. They are earnestly seeking answers.

Implication for South Africa

We in South Africa too have a porous border; but we have acted in a totally different and unacceptable way towards immigrants. The recent bouts of xenophobia have done lasting damage to our international reputation and our ability to absorb people from other countries. Furthermore, we have put at risk all those local companies that do business elsewhere in Africa. Apart from the senseless and brutal murders of innocent foreigners, the worst consequence is that so many talented foreign entrepreneurs have decided to quit this country and go back to their original home. They are fleeing the fury evident towards them in many communities around the country. No amount of conciliatory words are going to persuade them to stay as it can happen again. They are gone for good when, as I explained under the previous flag, the spark of entrepreneurship is the biggest determinant of the long-term economic fortunes of any nation and the biggest job creator.

Hence, we have to admit that the flag related to our own porous border is painted in stark colours as it is mixed with xenophobia of a violent nature. If we do not get our response right, South Africa will pay a very heavy price indeed. Worse still, xenophobia can descend into ethnophobia – the hatred of any race or ethnicity different to one's own – and that is when the game will really change. Meanwhile, the rich old millions in Europe and America have to review all their options to stem the flow of the poor young billions across their own boundaries.

Cybercrime and cyberterrorism

Cybercrime was the second biggest threat posed by the criminal world, according to the participants at the Interpol conference. It was acknowledged that the source of cyberattacks could alternatively be a gang of professional hackers linked to a terrorist organisation. The thing about this type of action is that it requires no physical presence at the scene of the crime. Borders are irrelevant. You can vault over them, care of the dark side of the world wide web. It is not like holding up a bank with guns. The money can be subtly removed over a period of time from customer accounts and in small enough individual amounts that escape immediate detection. In fact, the total sum stolen through cybercrime is now massively higher than through cash heists. Confidential data on clients can also be stolen as can internal emails, the latter kind of theft causing great embarrassment to Sony Pictures in Hollywood. Julian Assange and Edward Snowden have demonstrated the vulnerability of any communication between governments, and recently we had the case of a dating website being hacked by pro-fidelity activists. They gave the owners of the site an ultimatum to close down or risk the details of all their members being released to the public. Now they have done that.

A collection of ten mining flags

Next I would like to deal with a series of flags that are affecting the mining industry, the one that I have spent my life in. The currently depressed prices of most commodities conceal a critical change in the mining game. All the easy-to-find, easy-to-mine, easy-to-treat and close-to-customer mineral deposits have been found, mined, treated and despatched. The industry is in a much tougher state as indicated by my list of flags, below, concerning its future.

The first three flags I have already mentioned. The religious flag must make one cautious of entering countries divided by the flag. Where you have no choice because you are already there, it points to the need of having contingency plans to evacuate staff if necessary. The grey flag, and particularly in the way it affects China, suggests that the long boom of the last century is not about to be repeated. As one professional doomsayer said with a broad grin the other day: "Focus on what you think the global economic growth rate will be from here to 2050 and then halve your figure."

Productivity and keeping your costs down then become the key to a sustainable mining operation. The green flag could well affect the demand for thermal coal as nations seek to diversify their sources of energy and move away from the consumption of fossil fuels. It could also make water a more critical resource and its consumption subject to severe rationing. Mines would need to find smarter ways of using water and recycling it.

The fourth flag which is specific to the mining industry is resource nationalism, namely the desire by governments to have more control over deposits that lie in their territory. This may mean a partnership with government, as is the case with De Beers in Botswana, participation by local companies in the ownership of the mine, royalties on revenue in exchange for the government ceding the right to mine the deposit or simply a hike in the tax on mining profit.

The fifth flag is around community involvement and winning the hearts and minds of the people living in the vicinity of the mine. This demands a set of skills that extend beyond the mining and metallurgical disciplines.

The sixth flag relates to my opening paragraph in this section. New deposits are in remote places further from the customer. This complicates the feasibility study as it is not just about estimating the cost of establishing the mine itself. It may have to include the construction of a railway to get the ore to the coast and a port to ship the ore to the customer. A multitude of licences may be required as well. Recently, the serious write-down in value of several major projects being undertaken by the mining giants indicates the rising complexity of commissioning a new mine.

The seventh flag is around environmental impact, because new deposits are increasingly being found in ecologically sensitive areas. The assessment of the impact must now be seen as a truly independent, transparent one with absolutely no suspicion of interference by the party that wants to mine. Moreover, the preservation of a good corporate reputation rests on it being plain to see that every effort has been made to minimise environmental impact; and sometimes being willing to walk away from a project because the disturbance to nature completely outweighs the potential economic gain.

The eighth flag is around the rising standards demanded to ensure the safety and health of mining employees. The drive to reduce accidents, so that in the end mining is a zero-harm game, is unstoppable.

The ninth flag is one spotted by Pierre Wack during the 1970s. It is to do with a factor that aggravates the depth and length of a fall in price of any commodity. As the oil price fell, Arab countries tended to increase their oil production so that they could meet a fixed revenue target nationally. This created an even greater glut in the market, turning a mild decline in price into a massive shock. The same flag is driving the oil market today, but it also exists in the iron ore market for a different reason. In tough times, the major producers believe in maximising production to get as much as they can out of economies of scale. Hence, iron ore prices are likely to stay lower for longer than in the case of copper and nickel where the normal rules governing the equilibrium between supply and demand apply (a fall in price causes supply to fall, demand to rise and a recovery to set in). Thus, any commodity price projection should be influenced by the presence or absence of this flag.

The last flag is an interesting one and came from the conference that I attended in London in December 2014. Because the Earth has been scoured for the next big deposit of all metals many times over, it takes real imagination on the part of geologists to map out new areas with the chance of discovering that deposit. Nowadays, it may even lie on the ocean bed. Hence, one is beginning to see a division in the industry between exploration and mining. The former activity has become the playing field of the junior exploration companies where the geologists have an entrepreneurial approach because they will share in any bonanza made as a result of a new discovery. The find is then sold on to one of the major mining companies to exploit as they have the money and reservoir of skills to do so. Rio Tinto is encouraging this new form of relationship by offering to analyse, for free, existing and new drill cores brought to its laboratories by junior miners and prospectors. In the second half of this century when the world population measured in billions goes into double digits, a shortage of many minerals may well develop and lead to substitution by alternative natural and synthetic materials in more plentiful supply. Nevertheless, peak production of most commodities is well down the road, given the advances in mining and metallurgical technologies. Moreover, world consumption of energy and metals may one day peak as transport becomes more fuel-efficient, manufactured products are designed to have less material content and services grow as a percentage of the global economy.

The pandemic flag

There are plenty of reasons why this flag can shoot up at any time. It is a hybrid flag in that it is a clockwork flag around the trends that are increasing the likelihood of a pandemic, but it is a cloudy flag as to when a new pandemic will happen and how it will play out. Examples of past pandemics are the Black Death which killed somewhere between 75 and 200 million people between 1346 and 1353 and reduced the population in Europe by 30%; the Great Plague which caused the death of a quarter of London's population in 1665 and which was only halted by the Great Fire of 1666; and the Spanish Flu which killed 50 to 100 million people between January 1918 and December 1920 and reduced the world's population by 3 to 5%. In the latter case, the virus mutated during the pandemic into a much deadlier form.

An example of a current pandemic is HIV/AIDS. Since 1981, 39 million people have died from AIDS. At present

35 million people are living with HIV, of which 3.2 million are children. In my 1987 book, *The World and South Africa in the 1990s*, I said: "One of the disasters that can overturn any demographic projection is AIDS. Experts are working on a vaccine, but the problem is that the virus mutates. Hence, new strains arise, and this year's vaccine may not be effective against next year's virus. More importantly, the virus hits the immune system, which is the very thing that a vaccine is trying to strengthen to protect a person from catching the disease."

Medical scientists are still working on an effective vaccine; but they have managed to extend the lives of patients with the provision of antiretroviral drug therapy, effectively turning HIV into a chronic disease.

Many people were worried that the latest outbreak of Ebola, the epicentre of which was Guinea, Liberia and Sierra Leone, would turn into a pandemic. The fatality rate among those catching it was estimated to be 70%. But Peter Piot, the Belgian scientist credited with the discovery of Ebola in 1976 (it was named after a river in Zaire), made the following statement: "A mutation that would allow Ebola patients to live a couple of weeks longer is certainly possible and would be advantageous to the virus." Viruses want their carrier to survive long enough to spread.

It did not mutate this time around, so the outbreak was contained with a lot of external assistance being provided by the West. SARS (or Severe Acute Respiratory Syndrome) has often been mentioned as a candidate that could create a pandemic; and now we have MERS (or Middle East Respiratory Syndrome), a virus which has spread as far afield as South Korea.

So why is it more probable now that the pandemic flag could go up? There are many reasons. We now have much more international travel than before. Of course it can be stopped if a pandemic develops, but the risk is that an aggressive disease spreads so quickly that travel bans are implemented too late. The recent spate of migration to which I referred in the section on porous borders also increases the risk. Urbanisation has concentrated people into tens of millions in the major cities. Places like Tokyo, Mexico City, London, New York, Hong Kong and Sao Paulo are like dense and very dry forests where a small spark can trigger a catastrophe.

The over-prescription of antibiotics has induced genetic swaps and mutations in bacteria. Multi-drug resistant varieties of bacteria and viruses are a constant danger. For example, tuberculosis and malaria have developed multidrug-resistant strains. Climate change, by warming the globe, can spread bugs that are common in tropical areas to the regions further north and south. One must remember that the pandemic flag applies to fauna and flora as well. Intensive farming methods can accelerate the spread of certain viruses and certain swine flu strains can be transmitted to people with regular exposure to pigs. It is now believed by scientists that HIV is a virus that crossed the species barrier into humans.

Louis Pasteur outlined the worst case scenario for this flag when he said: "It is the microbes who will have the last word."

The internet and cellular flag

Technology is a clockwork flag once it is proven. One of the most interesting features of being a human being, who experiences a normal life span of three score years and 10 (or more), is the number of new technologies that completely transform your life. My grandfather was born in the 1880s when travel was restricted to ships, railways and horses. He lived long enough for cars and airplanes to make his travel plans vastly different. He actually toured the world with one of those enormous old cameras, taking pictures of people and landscapes. The telephone was invented shortly before his birth and became a universal means of communication during his lifetime. For my father, it was radio and television. I remember as a child watching the weekly situation comedy 'I Love Lucy' with him.

In 1925, the Russian economist, Nikolai Kondratiev, came up with the theory that long-term economic cycles were based on waves of technological innovations that occurred every 50 to 60 years. The latter created entirely new industries that went through an 'S' curve, signifying an initial period of adoption by pioneers, followed by a period of rapid growth as the popularity of the technology spread, and ending with growth diminishing as the market matured.

Steam power, railways and steel were succeeded by power stations; then the trio of the internal combustion engine, oil-based chemicals and synthetic materials; and more recently microelectronics and new devices for communication. The next wave has already started with biotechnology and genetic engineering.

So, in terms of my life, the biggest change has been the personal computer, the mobile phone and the internet. I no longer need the *Encyclopaedia Britannica* to look up facts. I just turn on my PC or iPad and type in the relevant word or phrase. Bingo! You get the answer. Dinner party conversations have been transformed as anything you say can be verified, or contradicted, instantly by one of your dinner companions checking on his or her mobile phone.

But the real changes flowing out of these new technologies have been in the business game. As an illustration, I ask myself: "Will newspapers go the same way as stagecoaches?" Stagecoaches as a means of travel between cities in England began in the 15th Century and reached their zenith from 1800 to 1830. Roads were smoother and eventually became tarred. This made travel more comfortable and faster. Allowing time for stops to change horses, average speeds for the journey went up to around eight miles per hour. London to York was shortened to a three-day adventure. Then along came a block-buster event – the establishment of railways in the 1840s which in terms of the old Standard Bank slogan were simpler, better, faster, while being cheaper too.

This caused a slump in the stagecoach industry from which it never recovered, other than as a romanticised legend in the hit movie *Stagecoach* made in 1939 and starring John Wayne. There was no reversion to the mean for the stage-coach as you see in economic cycles and stock markets. The game was over for good and the only use for stagecoaches after 1840 was as sporting and recreational vehicles. In the same way, ships were replaced by airplanes so ocean vessels are now most often used to carry freight and to go on cruises rather than to ferry passengers from one country to another.

The electronic headlines

The same thing that happened to stagecoaches and passen-ger ships is now happening to the printed newspaper indus-try. Around the world, the story is one of declining circulation and a fall in advertising revenue leading to a serious retrench-ment of reporters and other staff in the newsroom and else-where. Printing costs are being pared and overheads carefully scrutinised to eliminate what does not add value. This can all be traced to one simple fact: The public get their news vir-tually free of charge off the internet. In addition, they watch major news channels and share news on social media plat-forms.

As an article by Hugo Rifkind in *The Spectator* put it the other day, imagine a situation where one newspaper grabbed all the scoops and published them ahead of its competitors. Such is Google. We have moved from a situation where news of victory or defeat was conveyed by a rider on horseback; to newspapers dropped on your doorstep by young school children making some pocket money out of the newsagents; to news conveyed instantaneously by a click on the screen of a gadget sitting on your desk, in your bag or in your pocket. During the recent crisis in Greece, the stock markets ebbed and flowed within seconds of each twist and turn in the negotiations being revealed on the internet.

Moreover, on certain news websites you can comment on the news and be read by others as well. You can also participate in events as they unfold on Twitter. Even reporting news has become more democratic and affects the news itself. But for the fact that a policeman in America was filmed on a cell phone shooting a fleeing black man in the back, he would have probably gotten away scot-free. In the developing world, news travels very quickly by word of mouth from those who do have access to the internet to those who don't. Furthermore, the latest statistics on how many smartphones are now owned and being used in Africa are stunning and point to the fact that the smartphone is becoming the principal means of communication and information gathering on the continent. Lack of a fixed-line infrastructure has caused Africans to leap several generations of technology to satisfy their need to stay in touch.

Obviously, media groups are adjusting to the new reality; but a business model to ensure that a website can be truly profitable, as a newspaper once was, has yet to be developed. Some websites are free and earn their money through advertising, others restrict you to a limited number of views before you pay and some, like the *Financial Times*, make you pay up front. Even with these inconsistencies, the internet allows a person to travel around the world in 30 minutes to pick up the headlines on local newspaper websites. My favourites are *The Sydney Morning Herald*, *The Daily Telegraph* and *Los Angeles Times*.

Nobody is quite sure of the best model, but, having said that, some companies like Murdoch's BSkyB and South Africa's Naspers have wholeheartedly embraced the internet and satellite TV. They have built completely new businesses which are more profitable than even newspapers were in their heyday. On the other hand, the shake-up in the industry has already produced many victims around the world who, like the stagecoach companies, have packed up forever.

My own view is that newspapers can no longer compete on breaking news, but they can compete on commentary and entertainment. For example you do not buy *The Economist* to get the latest news, but to get an intelligent analysis of the news. Many Sunday newspapers are for browsing through and selecting articles which, in the normal course of events, you would not consider putting time into reading. Good columnists have become a key to keeping the loyalty of existing readers and attracting new ones. So, newspapers can still be a fascinating and absorbing experience that you cannot obtain by looking at a computer screen.

I just hope the CEOs and heads of strategy at the various newspaper groups in South Africa understand how much their game is changing as a result of the internet flag. It is ticking away in the background and becoming a more competitive clock. Moreover, to co-exist with internet, they are going to have to be foxes and carve out a new role for newspapers. I have met so many courageous journalists in this country who play an essential role in exposing malpractice wherever it exists and who spread the word on the pockets of excellence that we must replicate to be a winning nation. However, they need an environment which has a positive future and is not beset by commercial uncertainties and retrenchments. They need to travel in a modern vehicle capable of negotiating the challenging terrain ahead, not a stagecoach that can't.

The entrepreneur's paradise

The internet flag is allowing consumers to do more things for themselves in terms of booking a flight, hiring a car and finding a place to stay. The people who have come up with the new applications to enable this to happen have made a fortune, while those who have been disintermediated, because their layer of service is no longer required, have had to find a new purpose in life. Travel agents, for example, are more about offering expert advice than just booking tickets, and the same goes for estate agents. They are under much more pressure to add value as you can take a virtual walk around a house. Credit cards will possibly go the same way as cheque books – something you no longer regularly have on you – as mobile phones become electronic wallets which you use at the till. M-Pesa has fundamentally changed the payment process in Kenya. Transmitting money to your relatives in other countries can now be done by SMS. There is no need to go to the bank and make an electronic transfer. ATMs can now perform most of the functions previously done by tellers. Hence, branches of banks are being forced to change their roles to becoming more like advisory centres on money management. No wonder advances in technology disrupt the big hairy goals that boards of directors set for themselves.

For small business, the cellular flag is a total boon. All your marketing, ordering, administration and accounts can be done on a single device. New products can be promoted on social media. It has revolutionised the life of an entrepreneur who now has access to the entire global market via the internet. In the case of Chantell and myself, we could never have got into the consciousness of Americans with our foxy ideas 30 years ago. Now, care of the internet, they are one click away from our website just like South Africans. I find it perplexing that so many companies have websites that are frozen or ones that require a lot of effort to navigate and extract the relevant information from, when they should be at the core of their marketing and brand strategy.

The next flag in technology designed to transform our lives is just around the corner, if you buy into the Kondratiev wave theory. My bet is that we are going to move away from the area of communication to the field of alternative energy sources in light of climate change. Just as cellular phones meant it was no longer imperative for your house to be connected to telegraph wires, so home power units powered by solar panels on your roof will make you independent of the national power grid. Hurray!

The lifestyle and leisure flag

Because this flag is linked to the previous one, it is also a clockwork flag. When I see young people in a restaurant these days gazing at their smartphones rather than talking to their friends at the same table, I am reminded of pictures painted in Victorian times of young men and women earnestly reading letters from one another before replying to them. The telephone put that kind of written communication on the back burner for a century because you could ring up and talk. Now we are back to reading messages, albeit sent at a lower cost than snail mail and most likely costing less than a phone call. The more things change, the more they stay the same.

For me, though, the biggest consequence of the mobile phone is tilting the work-life balance towards work. When I was a young employee of Anglo American, you were expected to arrive at the office around 8am in the morning and leave around 6pm in the evening. Official working hours in head office were 8.30am to 5pm, with one hour for lunch. But most people who wanted to impress their boss did a slightly extra daily stint by arriving before him and leaving after him. When you got home in the evening, no thought of office matters was in your mind and it was pure family time until you went off to work the next day. When you went away on holiday for two or three weeks, it was a similar deal. Nobody phoned you up and no telex machine was anywhere to be seen at the seaside or in the bush to send you written messages. It was all play, no work.

Now, when I look at the younger generation, they are constantly at work. Much less time is allocated to pure play because the smartphone makes you accessible around the clock. Added to which there is a psychological condition called FOMO (or fear of missing out). Moreover, people expect you to respond to their SMSs and emails out of office hours, at the weekends and on holiday. I know you can put an automatic response on your email saying that you are out of the office, but the automatic reaction of the person trying to get hold of you is one of frustration. How dare you not be instantly at my beck and call. Have you lost the plot?

The reason I have included this flag is that it runs totally counter to the expectation people had about the changing nature of work in the 1960s. It was predicted that by the turn of the century we would be down to four-day working weeks as robots and computers would be taking the weight off our shoulders. We would be managing our leisure time, and what we did in it, as seriously as we managed our day at the office or plant. Now I know that more than ever many people work from home, which is part of the move away from formal to informal employment. But I do get the impression that young people work much longer hours in this century than they did in the last one and it puts a lot of stress on them.

The changing world of sport

What makes me think this way is a strategy session I attended recently where sport was involved. All along I have emphasised how different business is from sport. The rules of the former can change dramatically in a period of five to 10 years, whereas the rules of the latter stay virtually unchanged. Rugby, tennis, soccer and golf are played according to much the same rules as they were a hundred years ago. Dress code can change, but the game remains fundamentally the same. But what happens when a game of sport played in an unchanging way starts to decline in popularity among the public and begins to fade as a business?

In this regard, the flags are beginning to flutter in the breeze for golf. I watched a video at a friend's house while I was staying in London in December 2014. In it, it was said that two golf courses a week were closing down in America and slowly reverting to their natural state. You can see the odd one in South Africa doing the same. Jack Nicklaus was asked in the video how many new courses he was developing in America, and he fashioned his thumb and forefinger into a big fat zero and flashed it at the camera.

This chimes with an issue debated at a strategy session I conducted in the middle of 2015. It was for the management committee of a large residential estate in South Africa that has a golf course in the middle of it. The problem was that fewer people were playing golf each year even though they had done their best to organise company golf days. The revenue from green fees no longer covered the cost of maintaining the golf course so the non-golf-playing residents of the estate were being asked to chip in with additional levies. This move had obviously been greeted with dismay. The question put to the meeting was whether to close down the golf course and use the land to build more houses. They are currently mulling over the idea.

Rory McIlroy, one of the world's top golfers, spoke in the same vein about the future of golf. After losing out to Lewis Hamilton in the BBC Sports Personality of the Year Award in

December 2014, he was forced to admit that golf is not the force it used to be among young people. The principal reason is that they no longer wish to spend the time required to play a full round of 18 holes. They would rather be on their mobile phones learning some new application which gives them instant gratification. Moreover, golf is a relatively expensive game in terms of equipment and membership/green fees and we live in a world of economic hard times for all but the super-rich.

Simply put, golf is proving to be too time-consuming an experience for many potential newcomers and is pricing itself out of the market. Incidentally, sailing is to a certain extent suffering from the same condition. It too involves time and patience to rig the boat and when you get out into the ocean, there is no wireless connection for keeping in touch with your mates on the land. Bridge as a card game is on the same downward path, because thousands of hands have to be played in order to master it.

By contrast, cycling has grown immensely in popularity as a sporting pastime and so has jogging and walking. In these sports, you decide on how much time at the weekend you wish to pursue the activity and how much time to reserve for your family and other leisure activities. Cricket has changed its format, and rugby and soccer do not involve too many hours as a player or spectator. I guess also that contact sports still provide a thrill that wrestling with the contours of Mother Earth cannot offer. As someone once said, golf is a game involving one large and one small ball and the object is to hit the smaller one.

Various solutions are being put forward by the more audacious members of the American golfing community. The first is to make the cup on the green larger so that putting becomes easier and quicker. The second is to lower the number of holes per round from 18 to 12. One can imagine how these recommendations are viewed with horror by your average golf club member. A traditionalist will say that it is not the same game and that any fiddling with the format or the rules is out of the question. Yet, cricket did just that in order to survive and has become an enormously successful business in India in the relatively new 20/20 format.

Ironically, computerised golf, where you hit the ball off a mat at a picture and the computer calculates where your ball has landed and sets you up for the next shot, is now a flourishing business in shops in America. As someone who played golf for most of my life with a handicap in single figures, I have to say that I would get no pleasure out of this kind of indoor experience at all. Golf for me was about enjoying the fresh air and having a drink at the 19th hole afterwards in the pub.

So where does golf go from here? I would give anything to facilitate a strategic planning session with the US PGA and help them explore options to reinvent the game. I would even hold the flagstick! Gary Player once said that the more he practises, the luckier he gets. I would change the quote to the more you become a flagwatcher and think in a flexible way, the greater your chances of survival, providing you follow through like a fox.

The global scenarios

Given the 12 flags that I have specified as the ones to watch in capturing the possible highs and lows of the global game, what are the scenarios that Chantell and I are currently painting for the global economy? They are pictured in the matrix on the next page.

On the left of the horizontal axis is a 'U' denoting a long economic slog of at least five to 10 years before the world as a whole experiences a sustainable recovery. On the right is a 'V' where the recovery takes place much sooner during this de-

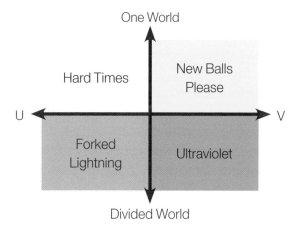

cade. On the upper part of the vertical axis is a world operating as one unit and, on account of globalisation, sharing a common destiny. At the bottom is a world that is becoming increasingly divided because of differing economic prospects, rising political tensions, creeping protectionism and regional strife.

Hard Times

Starting with the top left-hand quadrant and looking ahead for five years, 'Hard Times' is where the global economic growth rate does not meet expectations and the IMF keeps revising its estimate downwards. Virtually zero interest rates prevail as central bankers continue in their attempt to convert the mild recovery since 2008 into a full-blooded one, but much to their disappointment the economic pathway remains woefully flat. The US economy actually slows down in this scenario to an annual GDP growth of 2 to 3% because of the headwinds elsewhere in the global economy. The GDP of Europe and Japan remains stuck in the 0 to 1.5% annual growth range, China slows down to 5% and only a few African countries stay in the 7-8% bracket.

New Balls Please

'New Balls Please', to the right in the upper half of the matrix, takes its name from Wimbledon where the umpire calls for new balls during each tennis match. The title is to indicate that if the world is going to move onto a much higher plateau of economic growth, then the game requires new balls in the form of new technologies that create entirely new industries. As I mentioned earlier, the next Kondratiev wave could be around novel technologies harnessing fresh sources of energy, in particular ones that move the world away from fossil fuel consumption. It could also be around biotechnology/genetic engineering to create new medicines and plants; immuno-therapy to fight cancer; galactic tourism or space travel for ordinary people; driverless vehicles; and 3D printing. In the last regard, you may one day be able to gaze into a computer while it constucts a 3D image of yourself after which you press 'send' to be teletransported. 'Beam me up, Scotty' becomes a reality except that you should ensure beforehand that the re-cipient will not delete you! It might even be around irrigation and water management, as and when global warming makes water a scarcer resource. Whatever its nature, the wave hits faster than anticipated providing the kind of surge in the world economy that occurred in the 1950s. America's GDP jumps to an annual rate in excess of 5%, Europe and Japan hit 2-3% and China remains at 7%.

Ultraviolet

'Ultraviolet' (or 'UV' for short) in the bottom right-hand quad-rant presents a mixed picture: the 'U' of countries still stuck in the mire of zero to low economic growth; and the 'V' of countries whose economies are taking off towards the new boom of New Balls Please. This all happens against a back-drop of the increasing polarisation of nations into competing camps. For example, in this scenario there could be an American camp and Russian camp of allied countries facing off against one another. The only thing they have in common is the fierceness of their loyalties to each protagonist. Western economic sanctions would still be applying to Russia but the latter would be building up an alternative trading platform with its allies. In Ultraviolet, America's GDP grows at 4 to 5% per annum, Europe and Japan languish at 0-1.5% and China stays at 7%.

Forked Lightning

The last scenario in the bottom left-hand quadrant is 'Forked Lightning'. This is a double-dip scenario, namely a repeat of the 2008 financial meltdown except that the initiator is a major default on the national debt of a country, as opposed to a default on US sub-prime mortgages. Greek debt is too small for a default on it to initiate a global meltdown, but a default on, say, Spanish and Italian debt certainly qualifies. The default could be caused by a rise in interest rates, just as it did in 2008 when it made the mortgage debt unserviceable for many borrowers. In turn, the rise in interest rates could be caused by a rise in the inflation rate.

It should not be forgotten that the Wall Street Crash of 1929 was followed by another stock market crash in 1932. One of the consequences of historically low interest rates is that individuals and pension funds have had to diversify their portfolio of investments into the equity markets to make a sufficient return for their needs. They are therefore more exposed to downside risks and a dive in the markets associated with Forked Lightning. The alternative trigger for this scenario would be a further deterioration in the relationship between America and Russia with the real prospect of a war between the two.

The intuitive probabilities

Right now we are in the Hard Times scenario because America's GDP growth is forecast by the IMF to slow down to 2.5% in 2015, the Eurozone GDP growth rate is projected to be 1.5% and Japan's GDP growth rate 0.8%. China's GDP growth in 2015 is forecast to be 6.8%. Ultraviolet is the second most probable scenario to 2020 as one of the flags Chantell and I have had for a full blown recovery in the US is that the unemployment rate drops below 6%. Today it is 5.1%. It is therefore possible for the US economy to beat the IMF forecast of its growth rate in the near future, in which case we will be in the two-speed world of Ultraviolet. On the one hand, you will have China and America, the world's two largest national economies, looking fairly strong while Japan and the Eurozone lag behind because of the grey flag of ageing populations.

There is no sign yet of the technology revolution needed for New Balls Please so it is an outsider in the race to 2020. Perhaps the climate change summit in Paris in December 2015 will boost the potential emergence of a whole new set of industries based on clean green energy. That would increase the chances of the scenario materialising. Equally, no national debt default of magnitude is looming on the horizon and a war between America and Russia is improbable at the moment. So the odds which Chantell and I give to Forked Lightning are on a par with New Balls Please. Hence, the intuitive probabilities we attach to the four scenarios in the period to 2020 are 40% to Hard Times, 30% to Ultraviolet and 15% each to New Balls Please and Forked Lightning.

Chapter 3
The South African flags and scenarios

Bearing in mind the global flags and scenarios, what do our clients in South Africa feel about the possibilities for South Africa? There are eight flags and three scenarios. Before I deal with them, I would like to go back to my book *The World and South Africa in the 1990s* and revisit the portrait of a winning nation shown below.

PORTRAIT OF A 'WINNING NATION'

* High Education
* Work Ethic
* Mobilisation of Capital
* 'Dual-Logic' Economy
* Social Harmony
* Global Player

Education

On education, I said then: "On the brink of the knowledge-intensive 1990s, the foremost characteristic of a winning nation has to be the quality of its education system. I could have covered the chart with education, education, education and education. If you go to the Japanese and ask them 'What is the key to your success?', they will tell you that it is the uniformly high standard of education in Japan in both the rural and urban areas. Teaching is a much sought-after profession in Japan and pay compares well with the private sector. There are five applications for every teaching position. 90% of Japanese school children complete high school." The same could be said of Singapore, Hong Kong, Taiwan and South Korea which, as I mentioned in the preceding chapter, are the four new entrants to the super league of nations with per capita incomes above $35 000 a year. Educated tigers get rich.

Nearly 20 years later, the same principle of high quality education applies except that we have moved from the 'Age of Information' to the 'Age of Intelligence', on account of the internet essentially giving everybody who uses it instant access to knowledge and information. The differentiator now is the way we use the existing base of knowledge to dream up ideas that have not been dreamt up before. This is all about intelligence which means that teaching children cognitive skills is where the focus should be.

Francois Pienaar, the captain of our rugby team when we won the World Cup in 1995, is the driving force behind MAD or the Make a Difference Foundation. They raise money to send children from underprivileged backgrounds to good schools in South Africa. I have been the guest speaker at a few of his end-of-the-year functions to celebrate the progress made by the foundation. Several of the students are asked to reflect on their experiences in a short speech. They speak so well that you know that they are going to make an enormous contribution to society and be completely self-sufficient. The same goes for a brilliant school in Ottery, Cape Town, called Christel House. I did a talk there the other day at a fund-raising breakfast and some current pupils and one ex-pupil described how fortunate they had been to get the most important thing in life: a first-class education. The school is totally free of charge for the pupils, while the teachers are incentivised with bonuses for above-average performance.

Work ethic

The second condition for a winning nation is a strong work ethic but, as I said in 1987, there are four stipulations for people to be willing to work hard. The first is small government. I quoted a marvellous Chinese proverb: "Govern a great nation like you cook a small fish. Don't overdo it!" Government must act in a support role and be the servant of the people, not the other way around. Where government thinks of itself as the champion, the work ethic has declined. Crucially, the state has to have the right relationship with the private sector and allow entrepreneurs the freedom to generate their own wealth. Inherent in the journey of a developmental state that attains its goal of becoming a developed country is that it is a co-operative venture. The second stipulation for a work ethic is a sound family system and, as I said at the time, that relies on the migratory system in South Africa being phased out and better housing for poor families being provided. Since 1994, good progress has been made on this front.

The third stipulation contributing to work ethic is low taxation. If the marginal rate of taxation is higher than a certain percentage, people do not want to put in that extra effort because most of their additional income will go to the government. Moreover, countries compete for capable people to add to their 'knowledge armoury', and successful foreign companies to add to their economy. Low taxation rates are a primary source of attraction.

The fourth stipulation is absence of corruption. In those countries that go beyond a certain level of corruption whereby it seeps into every crevice, the general population becomes thoroughly demotivated as they see their hard-earned money disappearing in bribes. You have to have an open system with clear consequences for misbehaviour to minimise corruption in a country.

Mobilisation of capital

Having people who are well educated and work hard is not enough. One has to give them resources as well. Hence, the third factor that drives a winning nation is mobilisation of capital. For this to happen, you need to develop a national savings habit which requires positive real interest rates. One cannot ask people to save and in a year's time have them losing out in real terms. That is why, in the world at large, interest rates on bank deposits eventually have to rise to compensate for the rate of inflation. You cannot get around the classic macroeconomic equation – savings equals investment. Having obtained the savings, one must have a system that effectively delivers them to where they are most needed. One wants an environment in which anyone who wants to become a player and has spotted his niche in the market can gain access to the requisite financial resources. This particularly applies to the small-business and informal sectors of the economy. I will address this issue later on because we still have economic apartheid in South Africa.

Dual-logic economy

The fourth condition for a winning nation is to create a dual-logic economy. As I asserted earlier, new technologies have designed many workers out of the big business system. They, and new labour market entrants, will need to become entrepreneurs or join small businesses for their occupations. The only way to solve the problem is to promote the dual-logic economy which encourages big and small business into a symbiotic relationship and allows the wealth created in the first-logic economy of big business to be shared with the second-logic economy of small business. My company, Anglo American, has done pioneering work in this area with the successful implementation of the Zimele project. The main purpose of the project is to subcontract as many non-core

148

activities as possible of the group's mines to emerging new enterprises. With initial financial assistance from one of Zimele's six funds and professional advice from the Zimele team, the project has supported 1 855 companies, employing 38 000 people and with a combined turnover of R6 billion. Other big businesses should follow suit.

Social harmony

The fifth condition is a pretty obvious one: social harmony. You cannot have a divided team and be a winning nation. One of the reasons that Manchester United won every soccer trophy around with Alex Ferguson at the helm was that he kept the players united. An important implication of social harmony is that it cannot exist with either angry majorities or angry minorities. Nor can it exist with a grotesque level of inequality in society. As I maintained in the 1987 book: "This rule of the game signals that you must have a constitution acceptable to people as a whole." We now have that but we still have a long way to achieve social harmony.

Global player

Finally, it is those nations that look outwards that win. Nations that look inwards die. China has gone from the 100th economy in the world in 1978 to the second-largest economy today because they recognised this fact. After Mao Zedong's death, Deng Xiaoping succeeded him as China's leader and opened up the country to foreign investment and international trade. His favourite expression was: "I don't care if a cat is black or white as long as it catches mice." When I saw Nelson Mandela in prison in January 1990, he quoted those words to me. Another reason for being a global player is that you need enough exports to pay for your imports. Running a consistent current account deficit in the end does extensive damage to your currency.

We had an American expert helping our scenario team in the 1980s. He offered us an intriguing insight into his home country by asking us the following question: "Where does the Big Gorilla sleep?" The team responded: "In the grass." He said: "No." "In the cave?" "No." "In the tree?" "No." So we said, "We give up," and he said: "The Big Gorilla sleeps where he wants to sleep." The point of that statement was that America had behaved like the Big Gorilla for years and was under the impression it owned the whole jungle. Latterly, it has woken up to the fact that there are other players in the global game whose position has to be considered. In this regard, it is interesting to note that, despite low growth, the European Union's GDP of $18.5 trillion is currently higher than America's GDP of close to $18 trillion.

The eight South African flags

We now turn to the flags which concern our clients here, most of them being significant players in the private sector. All the flags are cloudy because they can lead the country in a multitude of different directions.

Corruption and crime

This is listed by our clients as the Number One flag to determine whether the country goes up or down with a capital 'C' for corruption and a small 'c' for crime. It ties in with a survey done by the Institute of Risk Management South Africa among the risk management and business community, and published in 2015. It too ranked corruption as the principal risk.

Three reasons are given for such a high ranking as either a flag or a risk. The first is that bribes (or as they are euphemistically called commissions) are an invisible tax and can suck the economy dry. Brazil's economic miracle has been savaged by corruption. The second reason is that most companies have corporate governance codes which directly forbid the practice of bribery. Apart from being immoral, bribes can irretrievably harm a company's reputation. In a worst case scenario, therefore, this flag can force international players of repute to quit South Africa. The third reason is that contracts are awarded to companies based on political connections rather than on price and ability to carry out the work. The result is that holes are beginning to appear in the country's infrastructure. As one member of the audience remarked: "We no longer drive on the left hand side of the road in some areas, but what is left of the road!"

Crime, and especially violent crime, is the cause of many talented South Africans, both black and white, emigrating from South Africa. It is also persuading enterprising foreigners to go home or not come here in the first place. Violent crime also has a direct impact on the quality of life of your average citizen who cannot afford to live in a walled estate. Fear is widespread and that is the antithesis of being a winning nation. The price of security is beginning to affect the economic competitiveness of many businesses. Accordingly, corruption and crime together constitute a major red flag for South Africa at the moment.

Quality of infrastructure

You cannot have a thriving private sector if the platform on which it is located is crumbling. This is why the state of our infrastructure rates as the second most important flag in determining our future. Of course, it is related to the first flag. Certainly, no parastatal company can provide an effective service if the turnover of directors on its board is excessively high. The latter situation conflicts with the company having a consistent strategy and tactics which ensure that it occupies a position on the upper half of our Business Gameboard. The current load-shedding saga is an excellent sub-flag to watch.

If Eskom begins to overcome its current operational problems by sorting out the maintenance backlog on its existing power stations and by commissioning its two new ones according to its latest schedule, this flag will start to go from red to green.

Style of leadership

Inclusive leadership is a necessary condition for being a winning nation. Lee Kwan Yew inherited a sad state of affairs in Singapore when he became Prime Minister in 1959. Through putting a great emphasis on education and law and order, he moulded a new nation intent on reaching for the stars. And by the time he retired as leader in 1990, they had got there. Nelson Mandela was the epitome of an inclusive leader. When I had five hours with him in his small cottage in the grounds of Victor Verster prison near Paarl, he blew me away with his passion for reconciliation. I thought he was going to ask me lots of difficult questions about the mining industry, instead of which he plied me with questions on the future of South Africa and whether it could become a winning nation. As we were saying goodbye to one another, he asked me to send his regards to Harry Oppenheimer because he respected him for being a business leader who had publicly opposed apartheid. As President of the country, he continued his ardent drive towards reconciliation. One of the most notable instances was his support of the Springbok rugby team in 2005, captured in the movie *Invictus*. I told Francois Pienaar that he was one up on me, because I had never been the real-life model for Matt Damon!

Unfortunately, Mandela's two successors haven't come close to being inclusive leaders and the tragedy is that we are probably more divided as a nation now than at any time since 1994. There is very little communication between government and business. Divisions exist within the tripartite alliance, and civil society is not being constructively engaged by the powers that be. Mandela's reign was truly a honeymoon period. I am afraid we may have to wait for the next generation of ANC leaders, who had nothing to do with the struggle, to find someone as powerful in bringing people together as Mandela was. Again, it's a crucial flag, as divided teams do not stay in the Premier League of nations.

Pockets of excellence

Like a Premier League soccer club needs its world-class stars to have any chance of ending the season in the top five, so a nation needs its pockets of excellence to be in contention on the world stage. In South Africa, this flag is green at the moment and shows we have a long way to fall if indeed we descend at all in the future. Our country is blessed with an extraordinary array of pockets of excellence. The country has world-class companies, private and state schools as good as any schools in the rest of the world and some outstanding universities, business schools and hospitals. The South African Revenue Service (SARS) is a world-class revenue collector. If pockets of excellence are used as examples to encourage the improvement of poorer performing institutions, and thereby lift the nation as a whole, the flag will remain green. If, however, obstructions are placed in their paths to reduce the appearance of elitism, it would be a leading indicator of embracing mediocrity – one of the worst flags of all.

Of the over 28 000 schools in South Africa, only about 5 000 are considered reasonable-to-excellent, and the balance of some 23 000 are rated dysfunctional-to-shocking. If those 5 000 excellent schools are dumbed down through, for example, insisting on an increase in class size, the country's long-term competitiveness will suffer a rude shock. The scale of the challenge in keeping the flag green is illustrated by the statistic that, in May 2015, South Africa was ranked second to last among 76 countries in terms of maths and science test scores obtained by 15-year-old learners. The survey was conducted by the Organisation for Economic Co-operation and Development.

Entrepreneurial spark

This flag is the one that changes the fortunes of nations the most. When I facilitate a strategy session in London, I sometimes ask the participants who put the 'great' into Great Britain. The answer I most often get is Queen Victoria. I say: "No, she was a consequence, not a cause." The people who made Great Britain great were all those humble scientists and entrepreneurs who invented among other things the steam engine, the flying shuttle and the spinning jenny and who hailed from Scotland, Birmingham, Manchester and Liverpool. They ushered in the Industrial Revolution in the second half of the 1700s which made Great Britain the richest nation on Earth by the 1850s, thus permitting Queen Victoria to rule so regally.

Look at the difference between North Korea and South Korea. Same people, same historic culture but South Korea's open democracy nurtured the entrepreneurs who created new car companies and Samsung. North Korea, otherwise known as the 'Hermit Kingdom', has done nothing except manufacture a nuclear weapon.

America understands all this. In order to stay the Number One economy on the planet, it knows that every generation has to produce hundreds of thousands of entrepreneurs among which are world-beaters like Henry Ford, Walt Disney, Bill Gates, Steve Jobs , Mark Zuckerberg and now South-African-born Elon Musk.

Musk began with developing Zip2 and PayPal as two popular internet sites; then founded SpaceX to manufacture space launch vehicles and reduce the cost of space travel for human beings; then expanded Tesla Motors into a leading maker of electric cars; then helped his cousins to establish SolarCity with the intention of making it one of the largest solar plants in the world. He has also laid the conceptual foundation for a Hyperloop train system which will reduce the travelling time between Los Angeles and San Francisco to 35 minutes. The train would be powered by linear induction motors and ride on an air cushion in a reduced pressure tube. It could thereby travel at speeds of around 1 000 kilometres per hour. Lastly, he has just unveiled a new lithium-ion battery to hang on your wall to power your home. In short, he is an entrepreneurial genius with a real talent for monetising scientific advances. Take a bow, Waterkloof House Preparatory School and Pretoria Boys High School where he was educated before leaving for Canada and then America.

South Africa has an ambivalent attitude towards entrepreneurs, even though its own destiny was transformed by all those diggers who swarmed to Kimberley for diamonds and the Witwatersrand for gold. The profit motive is reckoned by some people of left-wing persuasion to be evil. I always say to anybody who feels this way in the public sector that they draw a salary at the end of the month whereas an entrepreneur has to make a profit to put bread on the table. Family businesses are the same, even collectives.

One foreign investor told me the other day that they roll out the red carpet for him in other countries. In South Africa, they roll out the red tape! Bureaucracy here really cramps the style of entrepreneurs. One only has to think of what the new visa regulations have done to tourism. I would like our President, Jacob Zuma, to change the mantra from 'we need to create five million jobs by 2020' to 'we need to create one million new enterprises by 2020'. Given the flag around the changing nature of work, it is the only way to create five million jobs. Moreover, this is the best way to produce the 100 black industrialists that the government profoundly wishes to do as one of the features of the developmental state.

The irony is that the people who have done spectacularly well since 1994 in the entrepreneurial category are the Afrikaners. Necessity is the mother of invention because all their career entitlements fell away in that year. This should make one pause over the sense of entitlement fostered by black economic empowerment programmes, which admittedly are now broad-based. One does not want to undermine the creation of new black entrepreneurs. Much more important is to pull down the barriers which face many township entrepreneurs at the moment and which prevent them from spreading their wings in the mainstream economy.

Before concluding this section, it would be remiss of me not to mention Siyabulela Xuza who hails from the Eastern Cape. He has had a minor planet named after him by the MIT Lincoln Laboratory in America for the advances he has made in homemade rocket fuel. After studying at Harvard University, he is now back in South Africa looking at ways of storing energy in micro fuel cells. I want the climate for him, and all the bright South African inventors, to be one that spurs them to turn their ideas into successful business ventures. Our own industrial revolution will only happen under these circumstances.

Independence of judiciary and other institutions

This flag is green, although some of my colleagues feel it is yellow before turning to red like a traffic light. I am more positive as a flag normally measures the present situation, whatever the future holds. Right now South Africa has a whole bunch of vibrantly independent institutions which offset the power of government. It is not a dictatorship or even an authoritarian state like some other African countries. Moreover, we have the Constitution to protect those institutions.

Obviously, there is concern about some of the choices for leadership positions in the judiciary, but they are outnumbered by people of great integrity who are very effective in providing the checks and balances a modern democracy requires. The media is fiercely independent in its criticism of the government and big business; and we have a Competition Commission, Constitutional Court and a Public Protector of note. Whatever you feel about the trade unions, they too are formidable institutions in our society, even though – as I mentioned earlier – they face the possibility of declining membership.

But the flag demands that one keeps a wary eye out for, say, any move to gag the media or weaken the statutory bodies in a systematic sense. At the moment, it is a flag in South Africa's favour despite the examples of corruption we all know about. At least these are in the public domain.

Nationalisation

This is a rare example of a future flag, but it is such a red one that it justifies a mention. Beatrice Webb's nephew was an austere man called Stafford Cripps who became Chancellor of the Exchequer in 1947 in the Labour Government of Clem Atlee. He supported the nationalisation of coal, gas, steel, electricity, the railways, inland water transport, and health services. The only one of these that remains in state hands is the National Health Service which is a tribute to Cripps. The rest have been returned to private hands because they are better run that way.

For South Africa to go the route of nationalising the mines and banks, and maybe other industries as well, and expect a better outcome would be to defy history. I believe in economic freedom as strongly as the Economic Freedom Fighters but I differ completely in the tactics to achieve it. I don't think changing the ownership of the mines and banks will add one shred of economic freedom to the masses. And it won't add extra jobs either. The way to make it happen is to turn our thoroughly exclusive economy into an inclusive economy by levelling the playing field for small business and the informal sector. Steve Biko once said: "Handouts don't improve your

157

self-esteem. Doing it for yourself does." Nationalisation merely creates more people working for the state as opposed to working for themselves. It also transfers the risk of running a business to the state whereas taxing business is a risk-free activity. Moreover, the money raised by taxes should be spent on improving service delivery, not on gambling in the markets.

As one person put it to me, the idea of making government the centre of attention is like assuming tourists go to the game park to watch the rangers, not the wildlife. The rangers are only there to help the wildlife to thrive as the main attraction. The government should do the same for entrepreneurs in the real economy. They are the magnet for investment.

Land ownership

The final flag, despite being cloudy and uncertain, has aspects of a clock about it because it is a ticking time bomb. It is an inflammatory flag. It is the only flag that in a worst case scenario can ignite a civil war. It should be recalled that the Boers were winning the war in 1900 against the greatest imperial power at the time, Great Britain. Then along came Lord Herbert Kitchener who was utterly ruthless and implemented a strategy to make the Boer commandos surrender: the burning of their farms and the introduction of concentration camps in which over 26 000 women and children died. Concentration camps were a British, not a German invention. In this regard, I am disgusted by the country of my birth. The idea that a forceful seizure of the agricultural land will follow the Zimbabwean pattern and merely displace the current owners vastly underestimates their resolve to stay put. Equally, the idea that the status quo is sustainable is absurd. There has to be a more equitable distribution of the land between blacks and whites.

The other issue that cannot be sidestepped is food security. Of the 122 million hectares that constitute the total area of

South Africa, only 16.6 million hectares are considered arable, which means land that is suitable for dryland crop production without irrigation. That is 13.6%. Thus, the proposal that much of the land can be redistributed by dividing it up into smaller farms (or even subsistence units) ignores the fact that a farming region like the Karoo can only take a limited number of animals per hectare. It needs large farming units with economies of scale to make a profit. Putting more animals on the land will simply destroy it.

So the best case scenario for this flag is a mixture of dividing up the land where it can be done and collective ownership where it can't. Overarching any change is the need for financial and technical support for new black commercial farmers. Such a formidable problem can only be resolved with goodwill on both sides and some form of 'Agridesa' to negotiate a solution similar to the Codesa negotiations of the early 1990s. The current approach of one side putting up unilateral proposals for reforming land ownership and the other side defending the status quo at all costs is a dangerous non-starter.

The South African scenarios

Given the eight flags I have described, what are the latest scenarios to 2020 and the probabilities Chantell and I attach to them? Below is the matrix we have used for some time in presentations made to our clients.

The horizontal axis on the left depicts a situation where South Africa descends into conflict marred by violence and, in its extreme form, civil war and anarchy. On the right side, the axis represents South Africa at peace with itself and a model of social harmony. The upper half of the vertical axis is a country improving its competitiveness in the global game and reasserting itself as the premier economy in Africa. The lower half is a country declining in economic competitiveness where annual GDP growth is continually disappointing and at worst non-existent. This leads to three scenarios as it is impossible to be in the top left hand quadrant. A country cannot be riven by conflict and improving its competitiveness at the same time.

Premier League

'Premier League' is the name given to the scenario in the top right hand quadrant to imply that the competition between nations is just as deadly as the competition between the top soccer teams. In addition, citizens express patriotism for their country in the same way that fans demonstrate loyalty to their clubs. Just think of Russians versus Americans. It is an ongoing match which will probably go into extra time.

An annual league table is produced by the Institute for Management Development, a business school based in Switzerland and Singapore. It is called the World Competitiveness Yearbook and it is published in June of each year. The ranking is based on 300 criteria which measure how well a country is doing in managing its human and physical resources to facilitate long-term value creation. In 2015, the top five nations in the league of 61 nations were the United States, Hong Kong, Singapore, Switzerland and Canada. South Africa was ranked 53 between Jordan and Peru. Brazil was 56 and the bottom three places went to Argentina, Ukraine and Venezuela.

So, here we are as South Africa with the 33rd largest economy in the world; and yet we are ranked 20 places lower in what I call the Premier League of Nations. In 2010 we were 44 and now we have slumped to 53, close to the relegation zone. Going back to the brilliant diagram produced by Michael O'Dowd and Bobby Godsell which I showed at the beginning of the book, we are at the second crossroads. We reformed the politics and we must now remodel the economics, the exact opposite of the Chinese who transformed their economy and must now tackle their political system. In this scenario, we do just that by pulling down the silos in our economy and replacing economic apartheid with economic freedom for all.

Our economy is redesigned to unleash the entrepreneurial spirit and take our economic growth rate back up to 5% a year, the annual rate envisaged in the National Development Plan. Innovative solutions like virtual stock exchanges on the internet, similar to eBay but related to the buying and selling of shares in small business, are implemented in all our cities to liberate capital for entrepreneurs. The unused 2010 soccer stadiums are turned into open-air flea markets with different product lines on each floor: say restaurants on the top floor with a view, clothes on the second floor and, as somebody joked, guns and ammunition on the third floor to give the market a South African slant!

Our dilapidated infrastructure is restored to world-class standards and the checks and balances in our society which are laid down in our Constitution are strengthened. Corruption is rooted out and violent crime drops to a level which entices South African emigrants to come home. The ownership of land is sorted out in an amicable and productive manner. Pockets of excellence multiply, particularly in the field of education.

Second Division

In this scenario, we meander peacefully down into the 'Second Division' of nations, where we are treated like any other Third World country. We are not even aware of being relegated from the Premier League. Nigeria and other African nations are seen as the pioneers of the African entrepreneurial revolution and we are seen as a country still struggling with our past. BRICS might even become BRINC as we are replaced by Nigeria. Our economy remains stagnant and exclusive, with the wealth and income gap widening between ordinary citizens and the ultra-privileged coterie of the super-rich. Poverty, inequality and unemployment loom larger as a triple-headed monster. State interference in the economy increases in a vain attempt to rectify the situation.

Foreign investors stay away because of the uncertainties surrounding government policy towards business; and South African businesses switch their focus to markets beyond our borders on the African continent or relocate to overseas destinations. The number of talented young South African emigrants rises as they see limited prospects for themselves and their children by continuing to live here. Nothing too dramatic happens in this scenario and the same old South Africa bumbles into the future, albeit on a gently declining path.

However, it is a tough for government as they don't receive the tax revenue that they garnered in the Premier League and they don't have the same access to international capital as they currently enjoy – just when they have to finance the National Development Plan and National Health Insurance. Plans to expand our electricity and water supply to cater for the growth in population are postponed through lack of funds. Our bonds are downgraded to junk status by the ratings agencies and the rand exchange rate drops to a level where imported goods and overseas trips become outrageously expensive.

The real danger of this scenario is that the further down

the Second Division we go, the higher the risk of some random event propelling us into the next scenario which I will be describing. We lack the fortitude and resilience to recover from misfortune.

Failed State

This is the scenario where, in terms of the old expression 'adapt or die', we choose to die. Our ducks are neither in a row nor are they alive; they are buried six feet underground. The flag of violence and anarchy rises so high, we join the likes of Libya and Somalia in the perception of foreigners. Armed militias begin to displace government structures as old ethnic tensions return. The country descends into a perpetual state of civil war. Only a few pariah states welcome the turn of events but the rest of the word turns its back on us.

No expert in the field of political analysis has adequately described what a failed state or failing state would look like, or what the timing and rate of descent could be. Some deny that it could ever happen to South Africa, but the whole purpose of scenario planning is to examine the edge of the envelope. I can think of no rule of the game that rules out this scenario for South Africa, particularly if the land ownership issue is not resolved peacefully.

The intuitive probabilities

At the moment, we feel there is sufficient evidence in favour of the resilience of our democracy and the institutions that underlie it to allocate only a 10% probability to the 'Failed State' scenario. It is a wild card scenario or, as Malcolm Gladwell puts it, an outlier. Obviously, if the eight flags listed in the book turn a deeper shade of red or switch from green to red, then the probability of a Failed State outcome by 2020 will rise. That leaves 90% to be spread across Premier League and Second Division. We believe it is a 50/50 split between the two, so each scenario currently has a 45% probability. That is why we are at an economic crossroads and perhaps the only way to ensure we take the right path is to have an Economic Codesa, like the political ones we had in the early 1990s. On the other hand, I know some people argue that things never get accomplished here if the process is top down. Rather go for a bottom-up process by changing one community, region or city at a time. Whichever way one goes, the principle remains the same: hope for a positive future has to be accompanied by the effort to make it happen. All of us need to embark on a working journey, the name of the company I worked for in South Australia.

Conclusion

I have taken you in detail through the flagwatching methodology and given both global and South African examples of
flags. While I hope I have convinced you to aspire to being a
flagwatcher of note, it in no way displaces the art of scenario
planning. It modifies the order of the programme: you look
for the clockwork and cloudy flags changing the game around
you first and then play scenarios and attach probabilities as
best you can. You then decide on the best options and act accordingly. As I said earlier on, you may still prefer to use the
original foxy matrix contained in the *Mind of a Fox*; but the
new model puts flags at the forefront of figuring out what the
future holds in store.

   It is time for my last tribute to my late mentor, Pierre Wack,
and is a story I have told many times before. During my visit
to Boston in the 1980s, the professor in charge of the scenario
planning course, Bruce Scott, asked the two of us to his weekend retreat. It was February and bitterly cold. The countryside was covered in snow, which had been falling all week.
After a splendid meal in the evening, the host decided this was
a good moment to go tobogganing down the local country
lane. It was a long thin toboggan which at a pinch could
accommodate three people, in this case three scenario planners. So, in the pitch dark with Bruce lighting our way with a
torch, we walked to the top of the lane dragging the toboggan.
Bruce sat down at the front, with Pierre in the middle and
me at the rear. Bruce pointed the torch down the lane and we
set off.

The red flags were all at the top of the mast. The snow was beginning to turn to ice which meant the toboggan would gather speed very quickly. Second, visibility was virtually zero as the torch was a very poor substitution for car headlights. Third, two of the three passengers had no clue about the corners in this lane. Thus, the inevitable happened. Halfway down the lane, we missed a turn and plunged into a soft snowdrift. Luckily, none of us sustained serious injuries and our spirits were revived by the log fire and a nice glass of brandy back at Bruce's home. The moral of this story is that male bravado sometimes stands in the way of seeing the flags, even to those whose job it is to watch them.

While I have been writing this book, the future has been on display in all its sublety and ability to surprise. In particular, it has demonstrated how the interconnectedness of the flags can reshape the world. For example, the civil war in Syria is widely felt to be the principal cause behind the displacement of half of Syria's population of 23 million inhabitants. But the stress of extreme drought conditions has also taken its toll by forcing the Syrian people off the land into towns and greener pastures elsewhere. Hence, the religious flag has combined with the green flag to make the porous border flag the one that everybody is watching today. Moreover, as I hinted earlier, the great migration of the 21st Century may well lower the grey flag in receptive countries like Germany, as millions of young, potentially productive refugees travel by land and by sea to make a new life for themselves and their families there.

The bottom line is that decoding the future is a dynamic activity that never stops. It demands sharp eyes and an enquiring mind to detect the possibilities and a sufficient degree of nimbleness to cope with the consequences. It also demands a constant review of the flags as they rise and fall and the flexibility to revise the scenarios and probabilities in light of the evidence at hand. All these qualities are possessed by an experienced fox. Just be thankful that the future becomes the present and the present becomes the past. You can learn from your successes and mistakes in cracking the code and enhance your skills for the next instalment of the game. Practice makes better, but never perfect. That is why the future is so intriguing. There is no final answer.

Risk management is now a core discipline in most companies; and scanning the horizon for the flags that can upset the business is as important as auditing the integrity of its internal operating procedures. Sometimes the flags are so cloudy in their consequences that the normal distribution of probabilities represented by the bell curve goes out of the window. We move into the universe of 'fat tails' where the edges of the curve are thicker, and the statistically improbable becomes more likely. Flagwatching allows you to detect the tilt towards the unexpected as was the case with our capturing the possibility of 9/11 and the market crash of 2008. By using the technique described in this book, you can truly imagine the unimaginable and be better prepared for black swan events.

I would like to conclude with a line of a song by Bob Dylan which I used to sing in a folk duo at university and which captures the essential nature of the future: "The answer, my friend, is blowing in the wind, the answer is blowing in the wind." I wish you the best of luck in watching the flags to work out which way the wind is blowing. We do it with weathervanes in the physical world. Now you can do the same thing with the flags in your mind.

Acknowledgements

For the record I would like to mention the names of all the people who contributed to the scenario planning work I have done for the last 25 years. Firstly, as Chairman of Anglo American, Gavin Relly gave the go-ahead for scenario planning to be introduced inside the company in the early 1980s.

The consultants used in the original Anglo American exercise during the mid-1980s were Pierre Wack and Ted Newland (both formerly of Royal Dutch Shell), Edouard Parker, Hughes de Jouvenel, Michael Kaser, Henry Ergas and PA Technology.

The Anglo scenario team based in London who provided the content of the global scenarios for the original scenario exercise consisted of Luc Smets, Allan Newey, Yugo Kovach, Jackie Steinitz, Paul Missen and Ian Emslie.

The Anglo scenario team based in Johannesburg who provided the material for the South African scenarios consisted of Michael O'Dowd and Bobby Godsell, ably assisted by Michael Spicer, Jim Buys and Michael O'Connor. On the administration side, we had Gill Brown, Grace Sutherland and Muriel Cromey-Hawke, and for the translation into Afrikaans, Julia Viljoen.

For subsequent global scenario work, we added the following consultants: Heinrich Vogel, Alain de Vulpain, Michael Hinks-Edwards and Judie Lannon. We had friendly encouragement from Bruce Scott of the Harvard Business School and Peter Schwartz who succeeded Pierre as head of scenario planning at Shell. The London team was extended to include Steve Landsberg, Frank Meakin and Gil Devlin.

On the South African front, Margie Keeton, Gavin Keeton, Don Ncube and Colin Beeforth helped in updating the scenarios. Pat Meneghini and Drusilla Wildgoose assisted in the preparation of the manuscripts and graphics for our later exercises.

In relation to scenario workshops and research on the environment, valuable contributions were made by Brian Huntley, Roy Siegfried, Rick Lomba, Jock Danckwerts, Dave Dewar, George Ellis, Symonde Fiske, Tim Hart, Fred Kruger, Mike Mentis, Elize Moody, Graham Noble, John Raimondo, Roland Schulze, Butch Smuts, Rob Soutter, Jenny Thomson and Diana Banyard.

Enabling the material to be published in book form were Koos Human, Danie van Niekerk, Hans Buttner, Jürgen Fomm , Kerneels Breytenbach, Lappies Labuschagne, Linette Viljoen, Jill Martin, Erika Oosthuysen, Gerhard Mulder and in regard to this book, Annie de Beer, Andrea Weiss, Nazli Jacobs and Gill Moodie. Peter Gallo, Marie Bruyns and Brad Neal converted the content of earlier books into a video format. David Wightman, former editor of the Sunday Tribune, together with Cathryn Rees and Aneeqa Emeran of News24, allowed me to reach a wider audience with weekly columns on the future in a popular newspaper and on the internet.

In particular, I would like to pay tribute to Chantell Ilbury for sharing the design of a new model around the technique of scenario planning and her husband Daryl for giving us great insights and setting up our website. I also co-authored books with Brian Huntley, Roy Siegfried, Alan Whiteside and Wayne Visser.

To all of these people and the clients who have employed me to give presentations and facilitate strategy sessions, I am eternally grateful. May the fox be with you!

About the author

CLEM SUNTER was born in England and read politics, philosophy and economics at Oxford before moving to Zambia in 1971 to work for Anglo American Central Africa.

In 1973 he came to Anglo headquarters in South Africa, where he spent most of his career in the gold and uranium division, serving as its chairman and CEO from 1990 to 1996.

In the early 1980s, Sunter established a scenario planning function at Anglo with teams in London and Johannesburg. He is probably best known for his 'High Road/Low Road' scenarios for South Africa in the 1980s. His 2001 book, *The Mind of a Fox*, co-authored with Chantell Ilbury, anticipated a major terrorist attack on a western city before the 9/11 tragedy in New York. The book sold more than 50 000 copies.

Since 1987, Clem has authored or co-authored 18 books, many of them bestsellers. He has given scenario presentations worldwide, including lectures at the Harvard Business School in Boston and at the Central Party School in Beijing.

Sunter married Margaret Rowland in 1969 and they have one daughter and two sons. His hobbies include walking and rock music although he hung up his guitar professionally in 1964 shortly after his band played at the same gig as the Rolling Stones.

Books by the same author

The World and South Africa in the 1990s
South African Environments into the 21st Century (with Brian Huntley and Roy Siegfried)
The New Century
Pretoria will provide and other myths
The Casino Model
The High Road: Where are we now?
What it really takes to be World Class
Home Truths
Never mind the Millennium. What about the next 24 hours?
AIDS: The Challenge for South Africa (with Alan Whiteside)
The Mind of a Fox (with Chantell Ilbury)*
Beyond Reasonable Greed (with Wayne Visser)
Games Foxes Play (with Chantell Ilbury)*
Socrates & the Fox (with Chantell Ilbury)*
*Foxy Futurists & how to become one**
The Fox Trilogy (with Chantell Ilbury)*
*Calling all Foxes: Your time has come**
*21st Century Megatrends: Perspectives from a Fox**

* Also available as e-books.